THE

POETICAL AND DRAMATIC WORKS

OF

S. T. COLERIDGE.

WITH A MEMOIR.

VOLUME III.

BOSTON:
LITTLE, BROWN AND COMPANY.
NEW YORK: EVANS AND DICKERSON.
PHILADELPHIA: LIPPINCOTT, GRAMBO AND CO.
M.DCCC.LIV.

Entered according to Act of Congress, in the year 1854, by LITTLE, BROWN AND COMPANY, In the Clerk's Office of the District Court of the District of Massachusetts.

RIVERSIDE, CAMBRIDGE:
PRINTED BY H. O. HOUGHTON AND COMPANY.

STEREOTYPED BY STONE AND SMART.

CONTENTS.

VOL. III.

	Page
THE PICCOLOMINI; OR, THE FIRST PART OF WALLENSTEIN. A Drama. Translated from the German of Schiller	5
THE DEATH OF WALLENSTEIN. A Tragedy. In Five Acts	197
NOTES	327

THE PICCOLOMINI;

OR,

THE FIRST PART OF WALLENSTEIN.

A DRAMA.

TRANSLATED FROM THE GERMAN OF SCHILLER.

PREFACE OF THE TRANSLATOR TO THE FIRST EDITION.

THE two Dramas, PICCOLOMINI, or the first part of WALLENSTEIN, and WALLENSTEIN, are introduced in the original manuscript by a Prelude in one Act, entitled WALLENSTEIN'S CAMP. This is written in rhyme, and in nine syllable verse, in the same *lilting* metre (if that expression may be permitted) with the second Eclogue of Spenser's Shepherd's Calendar.

This Prelude possesses a sort of broad humour, and is not deficient in character; but to have translated it into prose, or into any other metre than that of the original, would have given a false notion both of its style and purport; to have translated it into the same metre would have been incompatible with a faithful adherence to the sense of the German, from the comparative poverty of our language in rhymes; and it would have been unadvisable from the incongruity of those lax verses with the present taste of the English Public. Schiller's intention seems to have been merely to have prepared his reader for the Tragedies by a lively picture of the laxity of discipline, and the mutinous dispositions of Wallenstein's soldiery. It is not necessary as a preliminary explanation. For these reasons it has been thought expedient not to translate it.

The admirers of Schiller, who have abstracted their conception of that author from the Robbers, and the Cabal and Love, plays in which the main interest is produced by the excitement of curiosity, and in which the curiosity is excited by terrible and extraordinary incident, will not have perused, without some portion of disappointment, the dramas, which it has been my employment to translate. They should, however, reflect that these are historical dramas, taken from a popular German history; that we must therefore judge of them in some measure with the feelings of Germans; or by analogy with the interest excited in us by similar dramas in our own language. Few, I trust, would be rash or ignorant enough to compare Schiller with Shakspeare; yet, merely as illustration, I would say that we should proceed to the perusal of Wallenstein, not from Lear or Othello, but from Richard the Second, or the three parts of Henry the Sixth. We scarcely expect rapidity in an historical drama; and many prolix speeches are pardoned from characters, whose names and actions have formed the most amusing tales of our early life. On the other hand, there exist in these plays more individual beauties, more passages, the excellence of which will bear reflection, than in the former productions of Schiller. The description of the astrological tower, and the reflections of the young lover, which follow it, form in the original a fine poem; and my translation must have been wretched indeed, if it can have wholly overclouded the beauties of the scene in the first act of the first play between Questenberg, Max. and Octavio Piccolomini. If we except the scene of the setting sun in the Robbers, I know of no part in Schiller's Plays which equals the whole of the first scene of the fifth act of the concluding play. It would be unbecoming in me to be more diffuse on this subject. A translator stands connected with the original author by a certain law of subordination, which makes it more decorous to point out excellences than defects: indeed he is not likely to be a fair judge of either. The pleasure or disgust from his own labour will mingle with the feelings that arise from an afterview of the original. Even in the first perusal of a work in any foreign language which we understand, we are apt to attribute to it more excellence than it really possesses, from our own pleasurable sense of difficulty overcome without effort. Translation of poetry into poetry is difficult, because the translator must give a brilliancy to his language without that warmth of original conception, from which such brilliancy would follow of its own accord. But the translator of a living author is encumbered with additional inconveniences. If he render his original faithfully, as to the sense of each passage, he must necessarily destroy a considerable portion of the spirit; if he endeavour to give a work executed according to laws of compensation, he subjects himself to imputations of vanity, or misrepresentation. I have thought it my duty to remain bound by the sense of my original, with as few exceptions as the nature of the languages rendered possible.*

It was my intention to have prefixed a Life of Wallenstein to this translation; but I found that it must either have occupied a space wholly disproportionate to the nature of the publication, or have been merely a meagre catalogue of events narrated not more fully than they already are in the Play itself. The recent translation, likewise, of Schiller's HISTORY OF THE THIRTY YEARS' WAR, diminished the motives thereto. In the translation I endeavoured to render my Author *literally* wherever I was not prevented by absolute differences of idiom; but I am conscious, that in two or three short passages I have been guilty of dilating the original; and from anxiety to give the full meaning, have weakened the force. In the metre I have availed myself of no other liberties than those which Schiller had permitted to himself, except the occasional breaking-up of the line by the substitution of a trochee for an iambus; of which liberty, so frequent in *our* tragedies, I find no instance in these dramas.†

---

* Originally prefixed to the translation of the second part, but apparently as a general introduction.

† Originally prefixed to the translation of the first part.

DRAMATIS PERSONÆ.

WALLENSTEIN, *Duke of Friedland, Generalissimo of the Imperial Forces in the Thirty Years' War.*
OCTAVIO PICCOLOMINI, *Lieutenant-General.*
MAX. PICCOLOMINI, *his Son, Colonel of a Regiment of Cuirassiers.*
COUNT TERTSKY, *the Commander of several Regiments, and Brother-in-Law of Wallenstein.*
ILLO, *Field-Marshal, Wallenstein's Confidant.*
ISOLANI, *General of the Croats.*
BUTLER, *an Irishman, Commander of a Regiment of Dragoons.*
TIEFENBACH,
DON MARADAS,
GOETZ,
KOLATTO,
} *Generals under Wallenstein.*
NEUMANN, *Captain of Cavalry, Aide-de-Camp to Tertsky.*
The War Commissioner, VON QUESTENBERG, *Imperial Envoy.*
GENERAL WRANGEL, *Swedish Envoy.*
BATTISTER SENI, *Astrologer.*
DUCHESS OF FRIEDLAND, *Wife of Wallenstein.*
THEKLA, *her Daughter, Princess of Friedland.*
THE COUNTESS TERTSKY, *Sister of the Duchess.*
A CORNET.
Several COLONELS *and* GENERALS.
PAGES *and* ATTENDANTS, *belonging to Wallenstein.*
ATTENDANTS *and* HOBOÏSTS *belonging to Tertsky.*
THE MASTER OF THE CELLAR *to Count Tertsky.*
VALET DE CHAMBRE *of Count Piccolomini.*

THE PICCOLOMINI.

ACT I.

SCENE I.—*An old Gothic Chamber in the Council-house at Pilsen, decorated with colours and other war insignia.*

ILLO *with* BUTLER *and* ISOLANI.

Illo. YE have come late—but ye are come!
        The distance,
Count Isolan, excuses your delay.
Iso. Add this too, that we come not empty
        handed.
At Donauwert * it was reported to us,
A Swedish caravan was on its way
Transporting a rich cargo of provision,
Almost six hundred waggons. This my Croats
Plunged down upon and seized, this weighty
        prize!——
We bring it hither——
Illo.   Just in time to banquet
The illustrious company assembled here.
But. 'Tis all alive! a stirring scene here!
Iso.   Ay!
The very churches are all full of soldiers.

* A town about twelve German miles northeast of Ulm.

And in the Council-house, too, I observe,
[*Casts his eye round.*

You're settled, quite at home! Well, well! we soldiers
Must shift and suit us in what way we can.

 Illo. We have the Colonels here of thirty regiments.

You'll find Count Tertsky here, and Tiefenbach,
Kolatto, Goetz, Maradas, Hinnersam,
The Piccolomini, both son and father——
You'll meet with many an unexpected greeting
From many an old friend and acquaintance. Only
Galas is wanting still, and Altringer.

 But. Expect not Galas.
 Illo. [*hesitating.*] How so? Do you know——
 Iso. [*interrupting him.*] Max. Piccolomini here?—O bring me to him.

I see him yet, ('tis now ten years ago,
We were engaged with Mansfeld hard by Dessau,)
I see the youth, in my mind's eye I see him,
Leap his black war-horse from the bridge adown,
And toward his father, then in extreme peril,
Beat up against the strong tide of the Elbe.
The down was scarce upon his chin! I hear
He has made good the promise of his youth,
And the full hero now is finished in him.

 Illo. You'll see him yet ere evening. He conducts

The Duchess Friedland hither, and the Princess
From Kärnthen. We expect them here at noon.

But. Both wife and daughter does the Duke
    call hither?
He crowds in visitants from all sides.
  Iso.   Hm!
So much the better! I had framed my mind
To hear of nought but warlike circumstance,
Of marches, and attacks, and batteries:
And lo! the Duke provides, that something too
Of gentler sort, and lovely, should be present
To feast our eyes.
  Illo. [*who has been standing in the attitude of meditation, to* BUTLER, *whom he leads a little on one side.*]   And how came you to know
That the Count Galas joins us not?
  But.   Because
He importuned me to remain behind.
  Illo. [*with warmth.*] And you?—You hold out
    firmly?
[*Grasping his hand with affection.*] Noble Butler!
  But. After the obligation which the Duke
Had laid so newly on me——
  Illo.   I had forgotten
A pleasant duty—MAJOR GENERAL,
I wish you joy!
  Iso.   What, you mean, of his regiment?
I hear, too, that to make the gift still sweeter,
The Duke has given him the very same
In which he first saw service, and since then,
Worked himself, step by step, through each pre-
    ferment,

From the ranks upwards. And verily, it gives
A precedent of hope, a spur of action
To the whole corps, if once in their remembrance
An old deserving soldier makes his way.

But. I am perplexed and doubtful, whether or no
I dare accept this your congratulation.
The Emperor has not yet confirmed the appointment.

Iso. Seize it, friend! Seize it! The hand which in that post
Placed you, is strong enough to keep you there,
Spite of the Emperor and his Ministers.

Illo. Ay, if we would but so consider it!—
If we would *all* of us consider it so!
The Emperor gives us nothing; from the Duke
Comes all—whate'er we hope, whate'er we have.

Iso. [*to* ILLO.] My noble brother! did I tell you how
The Duke will satisfy my creditors?
Will be himself my banker for the future,
Make me once more a creditable man!—
And this is now the third time, think of that!
This kingly-minded man has rescued me
From absolute ruin, and restored my honour.

Illo. O that his power but kept pace with his wishes!
Why, friend! he'd give the whole world to his soldiers.
But at Vienna, brother!—here's the grievance!—

What politic schemes do they not lay to shorten
His arm, and, where they can, to clip his pinions.
Then these new dainty requisitions! these,
Which this same Questenberg brings hither!—
  But.   Ay,
These requisitions of the Emperor,—
I too have heard about them; but I hope
The Duke will not draw back a single inch!
  Illo. Not from his right most surely, unless first
— From office!
  But. [*shocked and confused.*] Know you *aught*
    then? You alarm me.
  Iso. [*at the same time with* BUTLER, *and in a
hurried voice.*] We should be ruined, every one
    of us!
  Illo.   No more!
Yonder I see *our worthy friend* * approaching
With the Lieutenant-General, Piccolomini.
  But. [*shaking his head significantly.*] I fear we
    shall not go hence as we came.

SCENE II.—*Enter* OCTAVIO PICCOLOMINI *and* QUESTEN
BERG.

  Oct. [*still in the distance.*] Ay, ay! more still!
    Still more new visitors!
Acknowledge, friend! that never was a camp,
Which held at once so many heads of heroes.
                        [*Approaching nearer.*
Welcome, Count Isolani!

---

* Spoken with a sneer.

Iso.   My noble brother,
Even now am I arrived; it had been else my
      duty—
  Oct. And Colonel Butler—trust me I re-
      joice
Thus to renew acquaintance with a man
Whose worth and services I know and honour.
See, see, my friend!
There might we place at once before our eyes
The sum of war's whole trade and mystery—
[*To* QUESTENBERG, *presenting* BUTLER *and* ISOLANI *at the same time to him.*
These two the total sum—STRENGTH and DIS-
      PATCH.
  Ques. [*to* OCTAVIO.] And lo! betwixt them
      both experienced PRUDENCE!
  Oct. [*presenting* QUESTENBERG *to* BUTLER
and ISOLANI.] The Chamberlain and war-com-
      missioner Questenberg,
The bearer of the Emperor's behests,
The long-tried friend and patron of all soldiers,
We honour in this noble visitor.
                            [*Universal silence.*
  Illo. [*moving towards* QUESTENBERG.] 'Tis
      not the first time, noble Minister,
You have shown our camp this honour.
  Ques.   Once before
I stood before these colours.
  Illo. Perchance, too, you remember *where* that
      was.

It was at Znäim * in Moravia, where
You did present yourself on the part
Of the Emperor, to supplicate our Duke
That he would straight assume the chief command.
   Ques. To *supplicate?* Nay, noble General!
So far extended neither my commission
(At least to my own knowledge) nor my zeal.
   Illo. Well, well, then—to *compel* him, if you
       choose.
I can remember me right well, Count Tilly
Had suffered total rout upon the Lech.
Bavaria lay all open to the enemy,
Whom there was nothing to delay from pressing
Onwards into the very heart of Austria.
At that time you and Werdenberg appeared
Before our General, storming him with prayers,
And menacing the Emperor's displeasure,
Unless he took compassion on this wretchedness.
   Iso. [*steps up to them.*] Yes, yes, 'tis comprehensible enough,
Wherefore with your commission of to-day
You were not all too willing to remember
Your former one.
   Ques.   Why not, Count Isolan?
No contradiction sure exists between them.
It was the urgent business of that time
To snatch Bavaria from her enemy's hand;

---

* A town not far from the Mine-mountains, on the high road from Vienna to Prague.

And my commission of to-day instructs me
To free her from her good friends and protectors.
　Illo. A worthy office! After with our blood
We have wrested this Bohemia from the Saxon,
To be swept *out* of it is all our thanks,
The sole reward of all our hard-won victories.
　Ques. Unless that wretched land be doomed to
　　　　suffer
Only a change of evils, it must be
Freed from the scourge alike of friend and foe.
　Illo. What? 'twas a favourable year; the Boors
Can answer fresh demands already.
　Ques.　　　　　　　　　　　Nay,
If *you* discourse of herds and meadow-grounds—
　Iso. The war maintains the war. Are the
　　　　Boors ruined,
The Emperor gains so many more new soldiers.
　Ques. And is the poorer by even so many sub-
　　　　jects.
　Iso. Poh! we are all his subjects.　　[one fill
　Ques. Yet with a difference, General! The
With profitable industry the purse,
The others are well skilled to empty it.
The sword has made the Emperor poor: the plow
Must re-invigorate his resources.
　Iso.　　　　　　　　　　Sure!
Times are not yet so bad. Methinks I see
　　　　[*Examining with his eye the dress and ornaments of*
　　　　　QUESTENBERG.
Good store of gold that still remains uncoined.

Ques. Thank Heaven! that means have been
        found out to hide
Some little from the fingers of the Croats.
   Illo. There! the Stawata and the Martinitz,
On whom the Emperor heaps his gifts and graces,
To the heart-burning of all good Bohemians—
Those minions of court favour, those court harpies,
Who fatten on the wrecks of citizens
Driven from their house and home—who reap no
        harvests
Save in the general calamity—
Who now, with kingly pomp, insult and mock
The desolation of their country—*these*,
Let *these*, and such as these, support the war,
The fatal war, which they alone enkindled!
   But. And those state-parasites, who have their
        feet
So constantly beneath the Emperor's table,
Who cannot let a benefice fall, but they
Snap at it with dog's hunger—they, forsooth,
Would pare the soldier's bread, and cross his
        reckoning!
   Iso. My life long will it anger me to think,
How when I went to court seven years ago,
To see about new horses for our regiment,
How from one antechamber to another
They dragged me on, and left me by the hour
To kick my heels among a crowd of simpering
Feast-fattened slaves, as if I had come thither
A mendicant suitor for the crumbs of favour

That fall beneath their tables. And, at last,
Whom should they send me but a Capuchin!
Straight I began to muster up my sins
For absolution—but no such luck for *me!*
This was the man, this Capuchin, with whom
I was to treat concerning the army horses:
And I was forced at last to quit the field,
The business unaccomplished. Afterwards
The Duke procured me in three days, what I
Could not obtain in thirty at Vienna.

 Ques. Yes! your travelling bills soon
    found their way to us:
Too well I know we have still accounts to settle.

 Illo. War is a violent trade: one cannot always
Finish one's work by soft means: every trifle
Must not be blackened into sacrilege.
If we should wait till you, in solemn council,
With due deliberation had selected
The smallest out of four-and twenty evils,
I'faith we should wait long.—
"Dash! and through with it!"—That's the better
    watch-word.   [nature
Then after, come what may come. 'Tis man's
To make the best of a bad thing once past.
A bitter and perplexed "what shall I do?"
Is worse to man than worst necessity.

 Ques. Ay, doubtless, it is true: the Duke *does*
    spare us
The troublesome task of choosing.

 But.   Yes, the Duke

Cares with a father's feelings for his troops;
But how the Emperor feels for us, we see.
    Ques. His cares and feelings all ranks share
        alike,
Nor will he offer one up to another.
    Iso. And therefore thrusts he us into the deserts
As beasts of prey, that so he may preserve
His dear sheep fattening in his fields at home.
    Ques. [*with a sneer.*] Count, this comparison
        you make, not I.
    But. Why, were we all the Court supposes us,
'Twere dangerous, sure, to give us liberty.
    Ques. You have taken liberty—it was not given
        you.
And therefore it becomes an urgent duty
To rein it in with curbs.
    Oct. [*interposing and addressing* QUESTENBERG.] My noble friend,
This is no more than a remembrancing
That you are now in camp, and among warriors.
The soldier's boldness constitutes his freedom.
Could he *act* daringly, unless he dared
Talk even so? One runs into the other.
The boldness of this worthy officer,
                [*Pointing to* BUTLER.
Which now has but mistaken in its mark,
Preserved, when nought but boldness could preserve it,
To the Emperor his capital city, Prague,

In a most formidable mutiny
Of the whole garrison. [*Military music at a distance.*
Hah! here they come!

Illo. The sentries are saluting them: this signal
Announces the arrival of the Duchess.

Oct. [*to* QUESTENBERG.] Then my son Max.
too has returned. 'Twas he
Fetched and attended them from Kärnthen hither.

Iso. [*to* ILLO.] Shall we not go in company to
greet them?

Illo. Well, let us go.—Ho! Colonel Butler,
come. [*To* OCTAVIO.
You will not forget, that yet ere noon we meet
The noble Envoy at the General's palace.

[*Exeunt all but* QUESTENBERG *and* OCTAVIO.

SCENE III.—QUESTENBERG *and* OCTAVIO.

Ques. [*with signs of aversion and astonishment.*]
What have I not been forced to hear, Octavio!
What sentiments! what fierce, uncurbed defiance!
And were this spirit universal—

Oct. Hm!
You are now acquainted with three fourths of the
army.

Ques. Where must we seek then for a second
host
To have the custody of this? That Illo
Thinks worse, I fear me, than he speaks. And then
This Butler, too,—he cannot even conceal
The passionate workings of his ill intentions.

Oct. Quickness of temper—irritated pride;
'Twas nothing more. I cannot give up Butler.
I know a spell that will soon dispossess
The evil spirit in *him*.

   Ques. [*walking up and down in evident dis-
       quiet.*] Friend, friend!
O! this is worse, far worse, than we had suffered
Ourselves to dream of at Vienna. There
We saw it only with a courtier's eyes,
Eyes dazzled by the splendour of the throne.
We had not seen the war-chief, the commander,
The man all-powerful in his camp. Here, here,
'Tis quite another thing.
Here is no Emperor more—the Duke is Emperor.
Alas, my friend! alas, my noble friend!
This walk which you have ta'en me through the
       camp
Strikes my hopes prostrate.

   Oct.   Now you see yourself
Of what a perilous kind the office is,
Which you deliver to me from the Court.
The least suspicion of the General
Costs me my freedom and my life, and would
But hasten his most desperate enterprise.

   Ques. Where was our reason sleeping when we
       trusted
This madman with the sword, and placed such
       power
In such a hand? I tell you he'll refuse,
Flatly refuse, to obey the Imperial orders.

Friend, he *can* do't, and what he can, he will.
And then the impunity of his defiance—
O! what a proclamation of our weakness!

 Oct. D'ye think, too, he has brought his wife
   and daughter
Without a purpose hither? Here in camp!
And at the very point of time, in which
We're arming for the war? That he has taken
These, the last pledges of his loyalty,
Away from out the Emperor's domains—
This is no doubtful token of the nearness
Of some eruption!

 Ques.   How shall we hold footing
Beneath this tempest, which collects itself
And threats us from all quarters? The enemy
Of the empire on our borders, now already
The master of the Danube, and still farther,
And farther still, extending every hour!
In our interior the alarum-bells
Of insurrection—peasantry in arms——
All orders discontented—and the army,
Just in the moment of our expectation
Of aidance from it—lo! this very army
Seduced, run wild, lost to all discipline.
Loosened, and rent asunder from the state
And from their sov'reign, the blind instrument
Of the most daring of mankind, a weapon
Of fearful power, which at his will *he* wields!

 Oct. Nay, nay, friend! let us not despair too
   soon,

Men's words are ever bolder than their deeds:
And many a resolute, who now appears
Made up to all extremes, will, on a sudden,
Find in his breast a heart he knew not of,
Let but a single honest man speak out
The true name of his crime! Remember, too,
We stand not yet so wholly unprotected.
Counts Altringer and Galas have maintained
Their little army faithful to its duty,
And daily it becomes more numerous.
Nor can he take us by surprise: you know,
I hold him all encompassed by my listeners.
Whate'er he does, is mine, even while 'tis doing—
No step so small, but instantly I hear it.
Yea, his own mouth discloses it.

 Ques.   'Tis quite
Incomprehensible, that he detects not
The foe so near!

 Oct.   Beware, you do not think,
That I by lying arts, and complaisant
Hypocrisy, have skulk'd into his graces;
Or with the sustenance of smooth professions
Nourish his all-confiding friendship! No—
Compelled alike by prudence, and that duty
Which we all owe our country, and our sovereign,
To hide my *genuine* feelings from him, yet
Ne'er have I duped him with base counterfeits!

 Ques. It is the visible ordinance of heaven.

 Oct. I know not what it is that so attracts
And links him both to me and to my son.

Comrades and friends we always were—long habit,
Adventurous deeds performed in company,
And all those many and various incidents
Which store a soldier's memory with affections,
Had bound us long and early to each other—
Yet I can name the day, when all at once
His heart *rose* on me, and his confidence
Shot out in sudden growth. It was the morning
Before the memorable fight at Lützner.
Urged by an ugly dream, I sought him out,
To press him to accept another charger.
At distance from the tents, beneath a tree,
I found him in a sleep. When I had waked him,
And had related all my bodings to him,
Long time he stared upon me, like a man
Astounded; thereon fell upon my neck,
And manifested to me an emotion
That far outstripped the worth of that small service.
Since then his confidence has followed me
With the same pace that mine has fled from him.
 Ques. You lead your son into the secret?
 Oct.   No!
 Ques. What? and not warn him either what
  bad hands
His lot has placed him in?
 Oct.   I must perforce
Leave him in wardship to his innocence.
His young and open soul—dissimulation
Is foreign to its habits! Ignorance
Alone can keep alive the cheerful air,

The unembarrassed sense and light free spirit,
That make the Duke secure.
 Ques. [*anxiously.*] My honoured friend! most
   highly do I deem
Of Colonel Piccolomini—yet—if——
Reflect a little——
 Oct.   I must venture it.
Hush!—There he comes!

SCENE IV.—MAX. PICCOLOMINI, OCTAVIO PICCOLO-
   MINI, QUESTENBERG.

 Max. Ha! there he is himself. Welcome, my
   father!
 [*He embraces his father. As he turns round he observes*
   QUESTENBERG, *and draws back with a cold and*
   reserved air.
You are engaged, I see. I'll not disturb you.
 Oct. How Max.? Look closer at this visitor;
Attention, Max. an old friend merits—Reverence
Belongs of right to the envoy of your sov'reign.
 Max. [*drily.*] Von Questenberg!—Welcome—
   if you bring with you
Aught good to our head-quarters.
 Ques. [*seizing his hand.*] Nay, draw not
Your hand away, Count Piccolomini!
Not on mine own account alone I seized it,
And nothing common will I say therewith.
      [*Taking the hands of both.*
Octavio—Max. Piccolomini!
O saviour names, and full of happy omen!

Ne'er will her prosperous genius turn from Austria,
While two such stars, with blessed influences
Beaming protection, shine above her hosts.

   Max. Hey!—Noble minister! You miss your
       part.
You came not here to act a panegyric.
You're sent, I know, to find fault and to scold us—
I must not be beforehand with my comrades.

   Oct. [*to* Max.] He comes from court, where
       people are not quite
So well contented with the Duke, as here.

   Max. What now have they contrived to find out
       in him?
That he alone determines for himself
What he himself alone doth understand?
Well, therein he does right, and will persist in't.
Heaven never meant him for that passive thing
That can be struck and hammered out to suit
Another's taste and fancy. He'll not dance
To every tune of every minister.
It goes against his nature—he can't do it.
He is possessed by a commanding spirit,
And his too is the station of command.
And well for us it is so! There exist
Few fit to rule themselves, but few that use
Their intellects intelligently.—Then
Well for the whole, if there be found a man,
Who makes himself what nature destined him,
The pause, the central point to thousand thous-
       ands—

Stands fixed and stately, like a firm-built column,
Where all may press with joy and confidence.
Now such a man is Wallenstein; and if
Another better suits the Court—no other
But such a one as he can serve the army.
    Ques. The army? Doubtless!
    Oct. [*aside to* QUESTENBERG.] Hush! suppress
        it, friend!
Unless *some* end were answered by the utterance.—
Of *him* there you'll make nothing.
    Max.   In their distress
They call a spirit up, and when he comes,
Straight their flesh creeps and quivers, and they
    dread him
More than the ills for which they called him up.
The uncommon, the sublime, must seem and be
Like things of every day.—But in the field,
Ay, *there* the *Present Being* makes itself felt.
The personal must command, the actual eye
Examine. If to be the chieftain asks
All that is great in nature, let it be
Likewise his privilege to move and act
In all the correspondences of greatness.
The oracle within him, that which *lives*,
He must invoke and question—not dead books,
Not ordinances, not mould-rotted papers.
    Oct. My son! of those old narrow ordinances
Let us not hold too lightly. They are weights
Of priceless value, which oppressed mankind
Tied to the volatile will of their oppressors.

For always formidable was the league
And partnership of free power with free will.
The way of ancient ordinance, though it winds,
Is yet no devious way. Straight forward goes
The lightning's path, and straight the fearful path
Of the cannon-ball. Direct it flies and rapid,
Shattering that it *may* reach, and shattering what
    it reaches.
My son! the road, the human being travels,
That, on which BLESSING comes and goes, doth
    follow
The river's course, the valley's playful windings,
Curves round the corn-field and the hill of vines,
Honouring the holy bounds of property!
And thus secure, though late, leads to its end.

    Ques. O hear your father, noble youth! hear
        him
Who is at once the hero and the man.

    Oct. My son, the nursling of the camp spoke in
        thee!
A war of fifteen years
Hath been thy education and thy school.
Peace hast thou never witnessed! There exists
A higher than the warrior's excellence.
In war itself war is no ultimate purpose.
The vast and sudden deeds of violence,
Adventures wild, and wonders of the moment,
These are not they, my son, that generate
The Calm, the Blissful, and the enduring Mighty!
Lo there! the soldier, rapid architect!

Builds his light town of canvas, and at once
The whole scene moves and bustles momently,
With arms and neighing steeds, and mirth and quarrel
The motley market fills; the roads, the streams
Are crowded with new freights, trade stirs and hurries!
But on some morrow morn, all suddenly,
The tents drop down, the horde renews its march.
Dreary, and solitary as a church-yard
The meadow and down-trodden seed-plot lie,
And the year's harvest is gone utterly.

   Max. O let the Emperor make peace, my father!
Most gladly would I give the blood-stained laurel
For the first violet of the leafless spring,
Plucked in those quiet fields where I have journeyed!

   Oct. What ails thee? What so moves thee all at once?

   Max. Peace have I ne'er beheld? I *have* beheld it.
From thence am I come hither: O! that sight,
It glimmers still before me, like some landscape
Left in the distance,—some delicious landscape!
My road conducted me through countries where
The war has not yet reached. Life, life, my father—
My venerable father, life has charms
Which we have ne'er experienced. We have been

But voyaging along its barren coasts,
Like some poor ever-roaming horde of pirates,
That, crowded in the rank and narrow ship,
House on the wild sea with wild usages,
Nor know aught of the main land but the bays
Where safeliest they may venture a thieves' landing.
Whate'er in the inland dales the land conceals
Of fair and exquisite, O! nothing, nothing,
Do we behold of that in our rude voyage.

 Oct. [*attentive with an appearance of uneasiness.*] And so your journey has revealed this to you?

 Max. 'Twas the first leisure of my life. O tell me,
What is the meed and purpose of the toil,
The painful toil, which robbed me of my youth,
Left me a heart unsouled and solitary,
A spirit uninformed, unornamented.
For the camp's stir and crowd and ceaseless larum,
The neighing war-horse, the air-shattering trumpet,
The unvaried, still returning hour of duty,
Word of command, and exercise of arms—
There's nothing here, there's nothing in all this
To satisfy the heart, the gasping heart!
Mere bustling nothingness, where the soul is not—
This cannot be the sole felicity,
These cannot be man's best and only pleasures.

 Oct. Much hast thou learnt, my son, in this short journey.

Max. O! day thrice lovely! when at length the soldier
Returns home into life; when he becomes
A fellow-man among his fellow-men.
The colours are unfurled, the cavalcade
Marshals, and now the buzz is hushed, and hark!
Now the soft peace-march beats, home, brothers, home!
The caps and helmets are all garlanded
With green boughs, the last plundering of the fields.
The city gates fly open of themselves,
They need no longer the petard to tear them.
The ramparts are all filled with men and women,
With peaceful men and women, that send onwards
Kisses and welcomings upon the air,
Which they make breezy with affectionate gestures.
From all the towers rings out the merry peal,
The joyous vespers of a bloody day.
O happy man, O fortunate! for whom
The well-known door, the faithful arms are open,
The faithful tender arms with mute embracing.
  Ques. [*apparently much affected.*] O! that you should speak
Of such a distant, distant time, and not
Of the to-morrow, not of this to-day.

Max. [*turning round to him quick and vehement.* Where lies the fault but on you in Vienna?
I will deal openly with you Questenberg.
Just now, as first I saw you standing here,
(I'll own it to you freely,) indignation
Crowded and pressed my inmost soul together.
'Tis ye that hinder peace, *ye!*—and the warrior,
It is the warrior that must force it from you.
Ye fret the General's life out, blacken him,
Hold him up as a rebel, and Heaven knows
What else still worse, because he spares the Saxons,
And tries to awaken confidence in the enemy;
Which yet's the only way to peace: for if
War intermit not during war, *how* then
And *whence* can peace come?——Your own plagues fall on you!
Even as I love what's virtuous, hate I you.
And here make I this vow, here pledge myself;
My blood shall spurt out for this Wallenstein,
And my heart drain off, drop by drop, ere ye
Shall revel and dance jubilee o'er his ruin. [*Exit.*

Scene V.—Questenberg, Octavio Piccolomini.

Ques. Alas, alas! and stands it so?
[*Then in pressing and impatient tones.*
What, friend! and do we let him go away
In this delusion—let him go away?

Not call him back immediately, not open
His eyes upon the spot?

Oct. [*recovering himself out of a deep study.*]
  He has now opened mine,
And I see more than pleases me.

Ques.   What is it?

Oct. Curse on this journey!

Ques.   But why so? What is it?

Oct. Come, come along, friend! I must follow up
The ominous track immediately. Mine eyes
Are opened now, and I must use them. Come!
    [*Draws* QUESTENBERG *on with him.*

Ques. What now? *Where* go you then?

Oct.   To her herself.

Ques.   To——

Oct. [*interrupting him and correcting himself.*]
  To the Duke. Come, let us go—'Tis done, 'tis done,
I see the net that is thrown over him.
O! he returns not to me as he went.

Ques. Nay, but explain yourself.

Oct.   And that I should not
Foresee it, not prevent this journey! Wherefore
Did I keep it from him?—You were in the right.
I should have warned him! Now it is too late.

Ques. But *what's* too late? Bethink yourself, my friend,
That you are talking absolute riddles to me.

Oct. [*more collected.*] Come!—to the Duke's.
  'Tis close upon the hour

Which he appointed you for audience. Come!
A curse, a threefold curse, upon this journey!
[*He leads* QUESTENBERG *off.*

SCENE VI.—*Changes to a spacious chamber in the house of the* DUKE OF FRIEDLAND.—Servants *employed in putting the tables and chairs in order. During this enters* SENI, *like an old Italian doctor, in black, and clothed somewhat fantastically. He carries a white staff, with which he marks out the quarters of the heaven.*

1st Ser. Come—to it, lads, to it! Make an end of it. I hear the sentry call out, "Stand to your arms!" They will be there in a minute.

2d. Ser. Why were we not told before that the audience would be held here? Nothing prepared—no orders—no instructions—

3d. Ser. Ay, and why was the balcony-chamber countermanded, that with the great worked carpet?—there one can look about one.

1st. Ser. Nay, that you must ask the mathematician there. He says it is an unlucky chamber.

2d. Ser. Poh! stuff and nonsense! That's what I call a *hum*. A chamber is a chamber; what much can the place signify in the affair?

Seni. [*with gravity.*] My son, there's *nothing* insignificant,
Nothing! But yet in every earthly thing
First and most principal is place and time.

1st. Ser. [*to the second.*] Say nothing to him, Nat.
The Duke himself must let him have his own will.

Seni. [*counts the chairs, half in a loud, half in a low voice, till he comes to eleven, which he repeats.*]
Eleven! an evil number! Set twelve chairs.
Twelve! twelve signs hath the zodiac: five and seven,
The holy numbers, include themselves in twelve.
2d. Ser. And what may you have to object against eleven? I should like to know that now.
Seni. Eleven is—transgression; eleven oversteps
The ten commandments.
2d. Ser. That's good! and why do you call five a holy number?
Seni. Five is the soul of man: for even as man
Is mingled up of good and evil, so
The five is the first number that's made up
Of even and odd.
2d. Ser. The foolish old coxcomb!
1st. Ser. Ey! let him alone though. I like to hear him; there is more in his words than can be seen at first sight.
3d. Ser. Off, they come.
2d. Ser. There! Out at the side-door.
[*They hurry off.* SENI *follows slowly. A Page brings the staff of command on a red cushion, and places it on the table near the* DUKE's *chair. They are announced from without, and the wings of the door fly open.*

SCENE VII.—WALLENSTEIN, DUCHESS.

Wal. You went then through Vienna, were presented
To the Queen of Hungary?

Duch. Yes, and to the Empress too,
And by both Majesties were we admitted
To kiss the hand.

Wal. And how was it received,
That I had sent for wife and daughter hither
To the camp, in winter time?

Duch. I did even that
Which you commissioned me to do. I told them,
You had determined on our daughter's marriage,
And wished, ere yet you went into the field,
To show the elected husband his betrothed.

Wal. And did they guess the choice which I had made?

Duch. They only hoped and wished it may have fallen
Upon no foreign nor yet Lutheran noble.

Wal. And you—what do *you* wish, Elizabeth?

Duch. Your will, you know, was always mine.

Wal. [*after a pause.*] Well then,
And in all else, of what kind and complexion
Was your reception at the Court?

[*The* DUCHESS *casts her eyes on the ground and remains silent.*
Hide nothing from me. How were you received?

Duch. O! my dear lord, all is not what it was.
A cankerworm, my lord, a cankerworm
Has stolen into the bud.

Wal. Ay! is it so!
What, they were lax? they failed of the old
    respect?
Duch. Not of respect. No honours were omitted.
No outward courtesy; but in the place
Of condescending, confidential kindness,
Familiar and endearing, there were given me
Only these honours and that solemn courtesy.
Ah! and the tenderness which was put on,
It was the guise of pity, not of favour.
No! Albrecht's wife, Duke Albrecht's princely
    wife,
Count Harrach's noble daughter, should not *so*—
Not wholly so should she have been received.
    Wal. Yes, yes; they have ta'en offence. My
    latest conduct,
They railed at it, no doubt.
    Duch. O that they had!
I have been long accustomed to defend you,
To heal and pacify distempered spirits.
No; no one railed at you. They wrapped them
    up,
O Heaven! in such oppressive, solemn silence!—
Here is no every-day misunderstanding,
No transient pique, no cloud that passes over;
Something most luckless, most unhealable,
Has taken place. The Queen of Hungary
Used formerly to call me her dear aunt,
And ever at departure to embrace me—
    Wal. Now she omitted it?

Duch. [*wiping away her tears after a pause.*]
　　　　　　　　She *did* embrace me,
But then first when I had already taken
My formal leave, and when the door already
Had closed upon me, then did she come out
In haste, as she had suddenly bethought herself,
And pressed me to her bosom, more with anguish
Than tenderness.

　　Wal. [*seizes her hand soothingly.*] Nay, now
　　　　　collect yourself,
And what of Eggenberg and Lichtenstein,
And of our other friends there?

　　Duch. [*shaking her head.*]　　I saw none.

　　Wal. Th' Ambassador from Spain, who once
　　　　　was wont
To plead so warmly for me?—

　　Duch.　　　　　　　Silent, silent!

　　Wal. These suns then are eclipsed for us.
　　　　　Henceforward
Must we roll on, our own fire, our own light.

　　Duch. And were it—were it, my dear lord, in
　　　　　that
Which moved about the Court in buzz and whisper,
But in the country let itself be heard
Aloud—in that which Father Lamormain
In sundry hints and——

　　Wal. [*eagerly.*]　　Lamormain! what said *he*?

　　Duch. That you're accused of having daringly
O'erstepped the powers intrusted to you, charged
With traitorous contempt of th' Emperor

And his supreme behests. The proud Bavarian,
He and the Spaniards stand up your accusers—
That there's a storm collecting over you
Of far more fearful menace than that former one
Which whirled you headlong down at Regenspurg.
And people talk, said he, of——Ah!—

       [*Stifling extreme emotion.*

Wal.   Proceed!
Duch. I cannot utter it!
Wal.   Proceed!
Duch.   They talk——
Wal. Well!
Duch. Of a second——

     [*Catches her voice and hesitates.*

Wal.   Second——
Duch.   More disgraceful
——Dismission.
Wal. Talk they?

 [*Strides across the room in vehement agitation.*

    O! they force, they thrust me
With violence, against my own will, onward!
 Duch. [*presses near to him, in entreaty.*] O!
  if there yet be time, my husband! if
By giving way and by submission, this
Can be averted—my dear lord, give way!
Win down your proud heart to it! Tell that
  heart,
It is your sovereign lord, your Emperor
Before whom you retreat. O! let no longer

Low tricking malice blacken your good meaning
With abhorred venomous glosses. Stand you up
Shielded and helmed and weaponed with the truth,
And drive before you into uttermost shame
These slanderous liars! Few firm friends have
    we—
You know it!—the swift growth of our good fortune
It hath but set us up, a mark for hatred.
What are we, if the sovereign's grace and favour
Stand not before us?

SCENE VIII.—*Enter the* COUNTESS TERTSKY, *leading in her hand the* PRINCESS THEKLA, *richly adorned with brilliants.* COUNTESS, THEKLA, WALLENSTEIN, DUCHESS.

Coun. How, sister? What already upon business,

    [*Observing the countenance of the* DUCHESS.

And business of no pleasing kind I see,
Ere he has gladdened at his child. The first
Moment belongs to joy. Here, Friedland! father!
This is thy daughter.

    THEKLA *approaches with a shy and timid air, and bends herself as about to kiss his hand. He receives her in his arms, and remains standing for some time lost in the feeling of her presence.*

Wal. Yes! pure and lovely hath hope risen on
    me:
I take her as the pledge of greater fortune.

Duch. 'Twas but a little child when you de-
        parted
To raise up that great army for the Emperor:
And after, at the close of the campaign,
When you returned home out of Pomerania,
Your daughter was already in the convent,
Wherein she has remained till now.
    Wal.   The while
We in the field here gave our cares and toils
To make her great, and fight her a free way
To the loftiest earthly good; lo! mother Nature
Within the peaceful silent convent walls
Has done her part, and out of her free grace
Hath she bestowed on the beloved child
The godlike; and now leads her thus adorned
To meet her splendid fortune, and my hope.
    Duch. [*to* THEKLA.] Thou wouldst not have
        recognized thy father,
Wouldst thou, my child? She counted scarce
        eight years,
When last she saw your face.
    Thek.   O yes, yes, mother!
At the first glance!—My father is not altered.
The form that stands before me, falsifies
No feature of the image that hath lived
So long within me!
    Wal.   The voice of my child!
                    [*Then after a pause.*

I was indignant at my destiny
That it denied me a man-child, to be

Heir of my name and of my prosperous fortune,
And re-illume my soon extinguished being,
In a proud line of princes.
I wronged my destiny. Here upon this head
So lovely in its maiden bloom will I
Let fall the garland of a life of war,
Nor deem it lost, if only I can wreathe it
Transmitted to a regal ornament,
Around these beauteous brows.

[*He clasps her in his arms, as* PICCOLOMINI *enters.*

SCENE IX.—*Enter* MAX. PICCOLOMINI *and some time after* COUNT TERTSKY, *the others remaining as before.*

Coun. There comes the Paladin who protected us.

Wal. Max.! Welcome, ever welcome! Always wert thou
The morning star of my best joys!

Max.   My General——

Wal. 'Till now it was the Emperor who rewarded thee,
I but the instrument. This day thou hast bound
The father to thee, Max.! the fortunate father,
And this debt Friedland's self must pay.

Max.   My prince!
You made no common hurry to transfer it.
I come with shame: yea, not without a pang!
For scarce have I arrived here, scarce delivered
The mother and the daughter to your arms,

But there is brought to me from your equerry
A splendid richly-plated hunting dress,
So to remunerate me for my troubles——
Yes, yes, remunerate me! Since a trouble
It must be, a mere office, not a favour
Which I leaped forward to receive, and which
I came already with full heart to thank you for.
No! 'twas not so intended, that my business
Should be my highest best good fortune!

[TERTSKY *enters, and delivers letters to the* DUKE, *which he breaks open hurryingly.*

Coun. [*to* MAX.] Remunerate your trouble!
    For his joy
He makes you recompense. 'Tis not unfitting
For you, Count Piccolomini, to feel
So tenderly—my brother it beseems
To show himself for ever great and princely.

Thek. Then I too must have scruples of his love:
For his munificent hands did ornament me
Ere yet the father's heart had spoken to me.

Max Yes; 'tis his nature ever to be giving,
And making happy.

[*He grasps the hand of the* DUCHESS *with still increasing warmth.*

        How my my heart pours out
Its all of thanks to him: O! how I seem
To utter all things in the dear name Friedland.
While I shall live, so long will I remain
The captive of this name: in it shall bloom

My every fortune, every lovely hope.
Inextricably as in some magic ring
In this name hath my destiny charm-bound me!

Coun. [*who during this time has been anxiously watching the* DUKE, *and remarks that he is lost in thought over the letters.*] My brother wishes us to leave him. Come.

Wal [*turns himself round quick, collects himself, and speaks with cheerfulness to the* DUCHESS.]
Once more I bid thee welcome to the camp,
Thou art the hostess of this court. You, Max.,
Will now again administer your old office,
While we perform the sovereign's business here.

[MAX. PICCOLOMINI *offers the* DUCHESS *his arm, the* COUNTESS *accompanies the* PRINCESS.

Ter. [*calling after him.*] Max., we depend on seeing you at the meeting.

SCENE X.—WALLENSTEIN, COUNT TERTSKY.

Wal. [*in deep thought to himself.*] She hath seen all things as they are—It is so,
And squares completely with my other notices.
They have determined finally in Vienna,
Have given me my successor already;
It is the King of Hungary, Ferdinand,
The Emperor's delicate son! he's now their saviour,
He's the new star that's rising now! Of us
They think themselves already fairly rid,
And as we were deceased, the heir already

Is entering on possession—Therefore—dispatch!
> [*As he turns round he observes* TERTSKY, *and gives him a letter.*

Count Altringer will have himself excused,
And Galas too—I like not this!
   Ter.   And if
Thou loiterest longer, all will fall away,
One following the other.
   Wal.   Altringer
Is master of the Tyrole passes. I must forthwith
Send some one to him, that he let not in
The Spaniards on me from the Milanese.
——Well, and the old Sesin, that ancient trader
In contraband negotiations, he
Has shown himself again of late. What brings he
From the Count Thur?
   Ter.   The Count communicates,
He has found out the Swedish chancellor
At Halberstadt, where the convention's held,
Who says, you've tired him out, and that he'll have
No further dealings with you.
   Wal.   And why so?
   Ter. He says, you are never in earnest in your speeches,
That you decoy the Swedes—to make fools of them,
Will league yourself with Saxony against them,
And at last make yourself a riddance of them
With a paltry sum of money.

Wal.   So then, doubtless,
Yes, doubtless, this same modest Swede expects
That I shall yield him some fair German tract
For his prey and booty, that ourselves at last
On our own soil and native territory,
May be no longer our own lords and masters!
An excellent scheme! No, no! They must be off
Off, off! away! *we* want no such neighbours.
   Ter. Nay, yield them up that dot, that speck of
            land—
It goes not from your portion. If you win
The game, what matters it to you who pays it?
   Wal. Off with them, off! Thou understand'st
            not this.
Never shall it be said of me, I parcelled
My native land away, dismembered Germany,
Betrayed it to a foreigner, in order
To come with stealthy tread, and filch away
My own share of the plunder—Never! never!—
No foreign power shall strike root in the empire,
And least of all, these Goths, these hunger-wolves,
Who send such envious, hot and greedy glances
T'wards the rich blessings of our German lands!
I'll have their aid to cast and draw my nets,
But not a single fish of all the draught
Shall they come in for.
   Ter.   You will deal, however,
More fairly with the Saxons? They lose patience
While you shift ground and make so many curves.
Say, to what purpose all these masks? Your friends

Are plunged in doubts, baffled and led astray in
  you.
There's Oxenstein, there's Arnheim—neither
  knows
What he should think of your procrastinations.
And in the end I prove the liar; all
Passes through me. I have not even your hand-
  writing.

 Wal. I *never* give my hand-writing; thou
  knowest it.

 Ter. But how can it be *known* that you're in
  earnest,
If the act follows not upon the word?
You must yourself acknowledge that in all
Your intercourses hitherto with the enemy
You might have done with safety all you have done,
Had you meant nothing further than to gull him
For the Emperor's service.

 Wal. [*after a pause during which he looks narrowly on* TERTSKY.] And from whence dost *thou*
  know
That I'm *not* gulling him for the Emperor's service?
Whence knowest thou that I'm not gulling all of
  you?
Dost thou know *me* so well! When made I thee
The intendant of my secret purposes?
I am not conscious that I ever opened
My inmost thoughts to thee. The Emperor, it is
  true,
Hath dealt with me amiss; and if I *would*,

I could repay him with usurious interest
For the evil he hath done me. It delights me
To know my *power;* but whether I shall use it,
Of that, I should have thought that thou couldst speak
No wiselier than thy fellows.

 Ter. So hast thou always played thy game with us.   [*Enter* ILLO.

SCENE XI.—ILLO, WALLENSTEIN, TERTSKY.

 Wal. How stand affairs without? Are they prepared?

 Illo. You'll find them in the very mood you wish.
They know about the Emperor's requisitions,
And are tumultuous.

 Wal.   How hath Isolan
Declared himself?

 Illo.   He's yours, both soul and body,
Since you built up again his Faro-bank.

 Wal. And which way doth Kolatto bend? Hast thou
Made sure of Tiefenbach and Deodate?

 Illo. What Piccolomini does, that they do too.

 Wal. You mean then I may venture somewhat with them?

 Illo. —If you are assured of the Piccolomini.

 Wal. Not more assured of mine own self.

Ter.   And yet
I would you trusted not so much to Octavio,
The fox!

Wal.   Thou teachest me to know my man?
Sixteen campaigns I have made with that old
        warrior.
Besides, I have his horoscope,
We both are born beneath like stars—in short
                    [*With an air of mystery.*
To this belongs its own particular aspect,
If therefore thou canst warrant me the rest——

Illo. There is among them all but this one
        voice,
You *must* not lay down the command.   I hear
They mean to send a deputation to you.

Wal. If I'm in aught to bind myself to them,
They too must bind themselves to me.

Illo.   Of course.

Wal. Their words of honour they must give,
        their oaths,
Give them in writing to me, promising
Devotion to my service *unconditional.*

Illo. Why not?

Ter.   Devotion *unconditional?*
The exception of their duties towards Austria
They'll always place among the premises.
With this reserve——

Wal. [*shaking his head.*] All *unconditional!*
No premises, no reserves.

Illo.   A thought has struck me.

Does not Count Tertsky give us a set banquet
This evening?

Ter.   Yes; and all the Generals
Have been invited.

Illo. [*to Wallenstein.*] Say, will you here fully
Commission me to use my own discretion?
I'll gain for you the Generals' words of honour,
Even as you wish.

Wal.   Gain me their signatures!
How you come by them, that is *your* concern.

Illo. And if I bring it to you, black on white,
That all the leaders who are present here
Give themselves up to you, without condition;
Say, will you *then—then* will you show yourself
In earnest, and with some decisive action
Make trial of your luck?

Wal.   The signatures!
Gain me the signatures.

Illo.   Seize, seize the hour
Ere it slips from you. Seldom comes the moment
In life, which is indeed sublime and weighty.
To make a great decision possible,
O! many things, all transient and all rapid,
Must meet at once: and, haply, they thus met
May by that confluence be enforced to pause
Time long enough for wisdom, though too short,
Far, far too short a time for doubt and scruple!
This is that moment. See, our army chieftains,
Our best, our noblest, are assembled around you,
Their kinglike leader! On your nod they wait.

The single threads, which here your prosperous
    fortune
Hath woven together in one potent web
Instinct with destiny, O let them not
Unravel of themselves. If you permit
These chiefs to separate, so unanimous
Bring you them not a second time together.
'Tis the high tide that heaves the stranded ship,
And every individual's spirit waxes
In the great stream of multitudes. Behold
They are still here, here still! But soon the war
Bursts them once more asunder, and in small
Particular anxieties and interests
Scatters their spirit, and the sympathy
Of each man with the whole. He, who to-day
Forgets himself, forced onward with the stream,
Will become sober, seeing but himself,
Feel only his own weakness, and with speed
Will face about, and march on in the old
High road of duty, the old broad-trodden road,
And seek but to make shelter in good plight.
    Wall. The time is not yet come.
    Ter.   So you say always.
But *when* will it be time?
    Wal.   When I shall say it.
    Illo. You'll wait upon the stars, and on their
        hours,
Till the earthly hour escapes you. O, believe me,
In your own bosom are your destiny's stars.
Confidence in yourself, prompt resolution,

This is your VENUS! and the sole malignant,
The only one that harmeth you is DOUBT.
   Wal. Thou speakest as thou understand'st.
      How oft
And many a time I've told thee, Jupiter,
That lustrous god, was setting at thy birth.
Thy visual power subdues no mysteries;
Mole-eyed, thou may'st but burrow in the earth,
Blind as that subterrestrial, who with wan,
Lead-coloured shine lighted thee into life.
The common, the terrestrial, thou may'st see,
With serviceable cunning knit together
The nearest with the nearest; and therein
I trust thee and believe thee! but whate'er
Full of mysterious import Nature weaves,
And fashions in the depths—the spirit's ladder,
That from this gross and visible world of dust
Even to the starry world, with thousand rounds,
Builds itself up; on which the unseen powers
Move up and down on heavenly ministries—
The circles in the circles, that approach
The central sun with ever-narrowing orbit—
These see the glance alone, the unsealed eye,
Of Jupiter's glad children born in lustre.

    [*He walks across the chamber, then returns, and, stand-
      ing still, proceeds.*

The heavenly constellations make not merely
The day and nights, summer and spring, not
    merely
Signify to the husbandman the seasons

Of sowing and of harvest.   Human action,
That is the seed too of contingencies,
Strewed on the dark land of futurity,
In hopes to reconcile the powers of fate.
Whence it behoves us to seek out the seed-time,
To watch the stars, select their proper hours,
And trace with searching eye the heavenly houses,
Whether the enemy of growth and thriving
Hide himself not, malignant, in his corner.
Therefore permit me my own time.   Meanwhile
Do you your part.   As yet I cannot say
What *I* shall do—only, give way I will not.
Depose me too they shall not.   On these points
You may rely.
 Page [*entering.*] My Lords, the Generals.
 Wal. Let them come in.

Scene XII.—Wallenstein, Tertsky, Illo.—*To them enter* Questenberg, Octavio, *and* Max. Piccolomini, Butler, Isolani, Maradas, *and three other Generals.* Wallenstein *motions* Questenberg, *who in consequence takes the chair directly opposite to him; the others follow, arranging themselves according to their rank. There reigns a momentary silence.*

 Wal. I have understood, 'tis true, the sum and
   import
Of your instructions, Questenberg; have weighed
   them,
And formed my final, absolute resolve;
Yet it seems fitting, that the generals

Should hear the will of the Emperor from your
    mouth.
May't please you then to open your commission
Before these noble chieftains.
    Ques.   I am ready
To obey you; but will first entreat your Highness,
And all these noble chieftains, to consider,
The imperial dignity and sovereign right
Speaks from my mouth, and not my own pre-
    sumption.
    Wal. We excuse all preface.
    Ques.   When his Majesty
The Emperor to his courageous armies
Presented in the person of Duke Friedland
A most experienced and renowned commander,
He did it in glad hope and confidence
To give thereby to the fortune of the war
A rapid and auspicious change. The onset
Was favourable to his royal wishes.
Bohemia was delivered from the Saxons,
The Swede's career of conquest checked! These
    lands
Began to draw breath freely, as Duke Friedland -
From all the streams of Germany forced hither
The scattered armies of the enemy,
Hither invoked as round one magic circle
The Rhinegrave, Bernhard, Banner, Oxenstein,
Yea, and that never-conquered King himself;
Here finally, before the eye of Nürnberg,
The fearful game of battle to decide.

Wal. May't please you to the point.
Ques. In Nürnberg's camp the Swedish mo-
   narch left
His fame—in Lützen's plains his life. But who
Stood not astounded, when victorious Friedland
After this day of triumph, this proud day,
Marched toward Bohemia with the speed of flight,
And vanished from the theatre of war;
While the young Weimar hero forced his way
Into Franconia, to the Danube, like
Some delving winter-stream, which, where it
   rushes,
Makes its own channel; with such sudden speed
He marched, and now at once 'fore Regenspurg
Stood to the affright of all good Catholic Chris-
   tians.
Then did Bavaria's well-deserving Prince
Entreat swift aidance in his extreme need;
The Emperor sends seven horsemen to Duke
   Friedland,
Seven horsemen couriers sends he with the en-
   treaty:
He superadds his own, and supplicates
Where as the sovereign lord he can command.
In vain his supplication! At this moment
The Duke hears only his old hate and grudge,
Barters the general good to gratify
Private revenge—and so falls Regenspurg.
   Wal. Max., to what period of the war alludes he?
My recollection fails me here.

Max.   He means
When we were in Silesia.
 Wal.   Ay! Is it so!
But what had we to do *there*?
 Max.   To beat out
The Swedes and Saxons from the province.
 Wal.   True,
In that description which the minister gave
I seemed to have forgotten the whole war.
[*To* QUESTENBERG.] Well, but proceed a little.
 Ques.   Yes! at length
Beside the river Oder did the Duke
Assert his ancient fame. Upon the fields
Of Steinau did the Swedes lay down their arms,
Subdued without a blow. And here, with others,
The righteousness of Heaven to his avenger
Delivered that long-practised stirrer-up
Of insurrection, that curse-laden torch
And kindler of this war, Matthias Thur.
But he had fallen into magnanimous hands;
Instead of punishment he found reward,
And with rich presents did the Duke dismiss
The arch-foe of his Emperor.
 Wal. [*laughs.*]   I know,
I know you had already in Vienna
Your windows and balconies all forestalled
To see him on the executioner's cart.
I might have lost the battle, lost it too
With infamy, and still retained your graces—
But, to have cheated them of a spectacle,

Oh! *that* the good folks of Vienna never,
No, never can forgive me.
   Ques.   So Silesia
Was freed, and all things loudly called the Duke
Into Bavaria, now pressed hard on all sides.
And he *did* put his troops in motion: slowly,
Quite at his ease, and by the longest road
He traverses Bohemia; but ere ever
He hath once seen the enemy, faces round,
Breaks up the march, and takes to winter quar-
      ters.
   Wal. The troops were pitiably destitute
Of every necessary, every comfort.
The winter came. What thinks his Majesty
His troops are made of? Arn't we men? sub-
      jected
Like other men to wet and cold, and all
The circumstances of necessity?
O miserable lot of the poor soldier!
Wherever he comes in, all flee before him,
And when he goes away, the general curse
Follows him on his route. All must be seized,
Nothing is given him. And compelled to seize
From every man, he's every man's abhorrence.
Behold, here stand my Generals. Karaffa!
Count Deodate! Butler! Tell this man
How long the soldiers' pay is in arrears.
   But. Already a full year.
   Wal.   And 'tis the hire

That constitutes the hireling's name and duties,
The soldier's *pay* is the soldier's *covenant*.*

Ques. Ah! this is a far other tone from that,
In which the Duke spoke eight, nine years ago.

Wal. Yes! 'tis my fault, I know it: I myself
Have spoilt the Emperor by indulging him.
Nine years ago, during the Danish war,
I raised him up a force, a mighty force,
Forty or fifty thousand men, that cost him
Of his own purse no doit. Through Saxony
The fury goddess of the war marched on,
E'en to the surf-rocks of the Baltic, bearing
The terrors of his name. That was a time!
In the whole Imperial realm no name like mine
Honoured with festival and celebration—
And Albrecht Wallenstein, it was the title
Of the third jewel in his crown!
But at the Diet, when the Princes met
At Regenspurg, there, there the whole broke out,
There 'twas laid open, there it was made known,
Out of what money-bag I had paid the host.
And what was now my thank, what had I now,

---

* The original is not translatable into English;

——— Und sein *sold*
Mus dem *soldaten* warden, darnach heisst er.

It might perhaps have been thus rendered:

"And that for which he sold his services,
The soldier must receive."

But a false or doubtful etymology is no more than a dull pun.

That I, a faithful servant of the sovereign,
Had loaded on myself the people's curses,
And let the Princes of the empire pay
The expenses of this war, that aggrandizes
The Emperor alone—What thanks had I!
What? I was offered up to their complaints,
Dismissed, degraded!

   Ques.   But your Highness knows
What little freedom he possessed of action
In that disastrous diet.

   Wal.   Death and hell!
I had that which could have procured him free-
       dom.
No! Since 'twas proved so inauspicious to me
To serve the Emperor at the empire's cost,
I have been taught far other trains of thinking
Of the empire, and the diet of the empire.
From the Emperor, doubtless, I received this staff,
But now I hold it as the empire's general—
For the common weal, the universal int'rest,
And no more for that one man's aggrandizement!
But to the point. What is it that's desired of me?

   Ques. First, his imperial Majesty hath willed
That without pretexts of delay the army
Evacuate Bohemia.

   Wal.   In this season?
And to what quarter, wills the Emperor,
That we direct our course?

   Ques.   To the enemy.
His Majesty resolves, that Regenspurg

Be purified from the enemy, ere Easter,
That Luth'ranism may be no longer preached
In that cathedral, nor heretical
Defilement desecrate the celebration
Of that pure festival.

  Wal.   My generals,
Can this be realized?

  Illo.   'Tis not possible.

  But. It can't be realized.

  Ques.   The Emperor
Already hath commanded colonel Suys
To advance toward Bavaria!

  Wal.   What did Suys?

  Ques. That which his duty prompted. He advanced!

  Wal. What? he advanced! And I, his general,
Had given him orders, peremptory orders,
Not to desert his station! Stands it thus
With my authority? Is this th' obedience
Due to my office, which being thrown aside
No war can be conducted? Chieftains, speak
You be the judges, generals! What deserves
That officer, who of his oath neglectful
Is guilty of contempt of orders?

  Illo. [*raising his voice, as all but* ILLO *had remained silent, and seemingly scrupulous.*] Death.

  Wal. Count Piccolomini! what has he deserved?

  Max. Pic. [*after a long pause.*] According to the letter of the law,
Death.

Iso. Death.

But.   Death, by the laws of war.
    [QUESTENBERG *rises from his seat,* WALLENSTEIN
        follows; all the rest rise.

Wal. To this the law condemns him, and not I.
And if I show him favour, 'twill arise
From the rev'rence that I owe my Emperor.
   Ques. If *so*, I can say nothing further—*here!*

   Wal. I accepted the command but on con-
        ditions!
And this the first, that to the diminution
Of my authority no human being,
Not even the Emperor's self, should be entitled
To do aught, or to say aught, with the army.
If I stand warranter of the *event*,
Placing my honour and my head in pledge,
Needs must I have full mastery in all
The means thereto. What rendered this Gustavus
Resistless, and unconquered upon earth?
This—that he was the monarch in his army!
A monarch, one who is indeed a monarch,
Was never yet subdued but by his equal.
But to the point! The best is yet to come.
Attend now, generals!

   Ques.   The Prince Cardinal
Begins his route at the approach of spring
From the Milanese; and leads a Spanish army
Through Germany into the Netherlands.
That he may march secure and unimpeded,

'Tis th' Emperor's will you grant him a detach-
    ment
Of eight horse-regiments from the army here.
    Wal. Yes, yes! I understand!—Eight regi-
    ments! Well,
Right well concerted, father Lamormain!
Eight thousand horse! Yes, yes! 'Tis as it
    should be!
I see it coming.
    Ques.   There is nothing coming.
All stands in front: the counsel of state-prudence,
The dictate of necessity!——
    Wal.   What then?
What, my Lord Envoy? May I not be suffered
To understand, that folks are tired of seeing
The sword's hilt in *my* grasp: and that your court
Snatch eagerly at this pretence, and use
The Spanish title, to drain off my forces,
To lead into the empire a new army
Unsubjected to my control. To throw me
Plumply aside,—I am still too powerful for you
To venture that. My stipulation runs,
That all the Imperial forces shall obey me
Where'er the German is the native language,
Of Spanish troops and of Prince Cardinals
That take their route, as visitors, through the em-
    pire,
There stands no syllable in my stipulation.
No syllable! And so the politic court
Steals in a-tiptoe, and creeps round behind it:

First makes me weaker, then to be dispensed with,
Till it dares strike at length a bolder blow
And make short work with me.
What need of all these crooked ways, Lord Envoy!
Straight-forward, man! His compact with me pinches
The Emperor. He would that I moved off!—
Well!—I will gratify him!

   [*Here there commences an agitation among the* Generals *which increases continually.*

It grieves me for my noble officers' sakes!
I see not yet, by what means they will come at
The moneys they have advanced, or how obtain
The recompense their services demand.
Still a new leader brings new claimants forward,
And prior merit superannuates quickly.
There serve here many foreigners in th' army,
And were the man in all else brave and gallant,
I was not wont to make nice scrutiny
After his pedigree or catechism.
This will be otherwise, i' the time to come.
Well—me no longer it concerns.   [*He seats himself.*
  Max. Pic. Forbid it, Heaven, that it should come to this!
Our troops will swell in dreadful fermentation—
The Emperor is abused—it cannot be.
  Iso. It cannot be; all goes to instant wreck.
  Wal. Thou hast said truly, faithful Isolani!
What *we* with toil and foresight have built up,

Will go to wreck—all go to instant wreck.
What then? another chieftain is soon found,
Another army likewise (who dares doubt it?)
Will flock from all sides to the Emperor
At the first beat of his recruiting drum.

[*During this speech,* ISOLANI, TERTSKY, ILLO, *and*
MARADAS *talk confusedly with great agitation.*

Max. Pic. [*busily and passionately going from
one to another, and soothing them.*] Hear, my commander! Hear me, generals!
Let me conjure you, Duke! Determine nothing,
Till we have met and represented to you
Our joint remonstrances.—Nay, calmer! Friends!
I hope all may be yet set right again.

Ter. Away! let us away! in th' antechamber
Find we the others. [*They go.*

But. [*to* QUESTENBERG.] If good counsel gain
Due audience from your wisdom, my Lord Envoy!
You will be cautious how you show yourself
In public for some hours to come—or hardly
Will that gold key protect you from maltreatment.

[*Commotions heard from without.*

Wal. A salutary counsel——Thou, Octavio!
Wilt answer for the safety of our guest.
Farewell, Von Questenberg!

[QUESTENBERG *is about to speak.*

Nay, not a word,
Not one word more of that detested subject!

You have performed your duty—We know how
To separate the office from the man.

> [*As* Questenberg *is going off with* Octavio, Goetz, Tiefenbach, Kolatto, *press in; several other* Generals *following them.*

Goetz. Where's he who means to rob us of our
    general?

Tief. [*at the same time.*] What are we forced
    to hear? That thou wilt leave us?

Kol. [*at the same time.*] We will live with thee,
    we will die with thee.

Wal. [*pointing to* Illo.] There! the Field-
    Marshal knows our will.   [*Exit.*

> [*While all are going off the stage, the curtain drops.*

ACT II.

Scene I.—*A small Chamber.*

Illo *and* Tertsky.

Ter. Now for this evening's business! How
    intend you
To manage with the generals at the banquet?
  Illo. Attend! We frame a formal declaration
Wherein we to the Duke consign ourselves
Collectively, to be and to remain
His both with life and limb, and not to spare

The last drop of our blood for *him*, provided
So doing we infringe no oath nor duty,
We may be under to the Emp'ror.—Mark!
This reservation we expressly make
In a particular clause, and save the conscience.
Now hear! This formula so framed and worded
Will be presented to them for perusal
Before the banquet. No one will find in it
Cause of offence or scruple. Hear now further!
After the feast, when now the vap'ring wine
Opens the heart, and shuts the eyes, we let
A counterfeited paper, in the which
This one particular clause has been left out,
Go round for signatures.

  Ter.   How? think you then
That they'll believe themselves bound by an oath,
Which we had tricked them into by a juggle?

  Illo. We shall have caught and caged them!
        Let them then
Beat their wings bare against the wires, and rave
Loud as they may against our treachery,
At court their signatures will be believed
Far more than their most holy affirmations.
Traitors they are, and must be; therefore wisely
Will make a virtue of necessity.

  Ter. Well, well, it shall content me; let but something
Be *done*, let only some decisive blow
Set us in motion.

Illo. Besides, 'tis of subordinate importance
How, or how far, we may thereby propel
The generals.   'Tis enough that we persuade
The Duke, that they are his—Let him but act
In his determined mood, as if he had them,
And he *will* have them.   Where he plunges in,
He makes a whirlpool, and all stream down to it.

Ter. His policy is such a labyrinth,
That many a time when I have thought myself
Close at his side, he's gone at once and left me
Ignorant of the ground where I was standing.
He lends the enemy his ear, permits me
To write to them, to Arnheim; to Sesina
Himself comes forward blank and undisguised;
Talks with us by the hour about his plans,
And when I think I have him—off at once——
He has slipped from me, and appears as if
He had no scheme, but to retain his place.

Illo. He give up his old plans ! I'll tell you,
            friend !
His soul is occupied with nothing else,
Even in his sleep—They are his thoughts, his
            dreams,
That day by day he questions for this purpose
The motions of the planets——

Ter.   Ay ! you know
This night, that is now coming, he with Seni
Shuts himself up in the astrological tower
To make joint observations—for I hear,
It is to be a night of weight and crisis;

And something great, and of long expectation,
Is to make its procession in the heaven.

   Illo. Come! be we bold and make dispatch.
         The work
In this next day or two must thrive and grow
More than it has for years. And let but only
Things first turn up auspicious here below——
Mark what I say—the right stars too will show
         themselves.
Come, to the generals. All is in the glow,
And must be beaten while 'tis malleable.

   Ter. Do you go thither, Illo. I must stay
And *wait* here for the Countess Tertsky. Know,
That we too are not idle. Break one string,
A second is in readiness.

   Illo.   Yes! Yes!
I saw your lady smile with such sly meaning.
What's in the wind?

   Ter.   A secret. Hush! she comes.
                         Exit ILLO.

SCENE II.—(*The* COUNTESS *steps out from a Closet.*)
     COUNT *and* COUNTESS TERTSKY.

   Ter. Well—is she coming?—I can keep him
         back
No longer.

   Coun. She will be there instantly.
You only send him.

   Ter.   I am not quite certain
I must confess it, Countess, whether or not [know
We are earning the Duke's thanks hereby. You

No ray has broken from him on this point.
You have o'er-ruled me, and yourself know best,
How far you dare proceed.
 Coun.   I take it on me.
    [*Talking to herself, while she is advancing.*
Here's no need of full powers and commissions—
My cloudy Duke! we understand each other—
And without words. What, could I not unriddle,
Wherefore the daughter should be sent for hither,
Why first *he*, and no other, should be chosen
To fetch her hither! This sham of betrothing her
To a bridegroom,* whom no one knows—No!
   no!——
This may blind others? I see through thee,
   Brother!
But it beseems thee not, to draw a card
At such a game. Not yet!—It all remains
Mutely delivered up to my finessing——
Well—thou shalt not have been deceived, Duke
   Friedland!
In her who is thy sister.——
 Servant [*enters.*] The commanders!
 Ter. [*to the Countess.*] Take care you heat his
   fancy and affections—
Possess him with a reverie, and send him,

---

* In Germany, after honourable addresses have been paid and formally accepted, the lovers are called Bride and Bridegroom, even though the marriage should not take place till years afterwards.

Absent and dreaming, to the banquet; that
He may not boggle at the signature.

Coun. Take you care of your guests!—Go,
send him hither.

Ter. All rests upon his undersigning.

Coun. [*interrupting him.*] Go to your guests!
Go——

Illo. [*comes back.*] Where art staying, Tertsky?
The house is full, and all expecting you.

Ter. Instantly! Instantly! [*To the* Countess.]
And let him not
Stay here too long. It might awake suspicion
In the old man———

Coun. A truce with your precautions!

[*Exeunt* Tertsky *and* Illo.

Scene III.—Countess, Max. Piccolomini.

Max. [*peeping in on the stage, slily.*] Aunt
Tertsky! may I venture?

[*Advances to the middle of the stage, and looks around him with uneasiness.*

She's not here!
Where is she?

Coun. Look but somewhat narrowly
In yonder corner, lest perhaps she lie
Concealed behind that screen.

Max. There lie her gloves!

[*Snatches at them, but the* Countess *takes them herself.*

You unkind lady! You refuse me this—
You make it an amusement to torment me.

Coun. And this the thanks you give me for my
    trouble?
Max. O, if you felt the oppression at *my*
    heart!
Since we've been here, so to constrain myself—
With such poor stealth to hazard words and
    glances—
These, these are not my habits!
    Coun.   You have still
Many new habits to acquire, young friend!
But on this proof of your obedient temper
I must continue to insist; and only
On this condition can I play the agent
For your concerns.
    Max.   But wherefore comes she not?
Where is she?
    Coun.   Into *my* hands you must place it
Whole and entire. Whom could you find, indeed,
More zealously affected to your interest?
No soul on earth must know it—not your father.
He must not above all.
    Max.   Alas! what danger?
Here is no face on which I might concentre
All the enraptured soul stirs up within me.
O lady! tell me. Is all changed around me?
Or is it only I?
            I find myself
As among strangers! Not a trace is left
Of all my former wishes, former joys.
Where has it vanished to? There was a time

When even, methought, with such a world as this
I was not discontented.   Now how flat!
How stale!   No life, no bloom, no flavour in it!
My comrades are intolerable to me.
My father—Even to him I can say nothing.
My arms, my military duties—O!
They are such wearying toys!
 Coun.   But, gentle friend!
I must entreat it of your condescension,
You would be pleased to sink your eye, and favour
With one short glance or two this poor stale world
Where even now much, and of much moment,
Is on the eve of its completion.
 Max.   Something,
I can't but know, is going forward round me.
I see it gathering, crowding, driving on,
In wild uncustomary movements.   Well,
In due time, doubtless, it will reach even me.
Where think you I have been, dear lady?   Nay,
No raillery.   The turmoil of the camp,
The spring-tide of acquaintance rolling in,
The pointless jest, the empty conversation,
Oppressed and stifled me.   I gasped for air—
I could not breathe—I was constrained to fly,
To seek a silence out for my full heart;
And a pure spot wherein to feel my happiness.
No smiling, Countess!   In the church was I.
There is a cloister here to the * heaven's gate,

---

 * I am doubtful whether this be the dedication of the cloister or the name of one of the city gates, near which it stood.

Thither I went, there found myself alone.
Over the altar hung a holy mother;
A wretched painting 'twas, yet 'twas the friend
That I was seeking in this moment. Ah,
How oft have I beheld that glorious form
In splendour, 'mid ecstatic worshippers,
Yet, still it moved me not! and now at once
Was my devotion cloudless as my love.

  Coun. Enjoy your fortune and felicity!
Forget the world around you. Meantime, friend-
        ship
Shall keep strict vigils for you, anxious, active.
Only be manageable when that friendship
Points you the road to full accomplishment.
How long may it be since you declared your
        passion?

  Max. This morning did I hazard the first word.

  Coun. This morning the first time in twenty
        days?

  Max. 'Twas at that hunting-castle, betwixt here
And Nepomuck, where *you* had joined us, and—
That was the last relay of the whole journey!
In a balcony we were standing mute,
And gazing out upon the dreary field:
Before us the dragoons were riding onward,
The safe-guard which the Duke had sent us—
        heavy

I have translated it in the former sense; but fearful of having made some blunder, I add the original.—Es ist ein Kloster hier *zur Himmelspforte.*

The inquietude of parting lay upon me,
And trembling ventured I at length these words:
This all reminds me, noble maiden, that
To-day, I must take leave of my good fortune.
A few hours more, and you will find a father,
Will see yourself surrounded by new friends,
And I henceforth shall be but as a stranger,
Lost in the many—" Speak with my Aunt
    Tertsky!"
With hurrying voice she interrupted me.
She faltered. I beheld a glowing red
Possess her beautiful cheeks, and from the ground
Raised slowly up her eye met mine—no longer
Did I control myself.

    [*The* PRINCESS THEKLA *appears at the door, and remains standing, observed by the* COUNTESS, *but not by* PICCOLOMINI.

                        With instant boldness
I caught her in my arms, my mouth touched hers;
There was a rustling in the room close by;
It parted us—'Twas you. What since has
    happened,
You know.

    Coun. [*after a pause, with a stolen glance at* THEKLA.] And is it your excess of modesty;
Or are you so incurious, that you do not
Ask me too of my secret?

    Max.   Of *your* secret?

    Coun. Why, yes! When in the instant after you
I stepped into the room, and found my niece there,

What she in this first moment of the heart
Ta'en with surprise—
  Max. [*with eagerness*] Well.

Scene IV.—Thekla (*hurries forward,*) Countess, Max.
                   Piccolomini.

  Thek. [*to the* Countess.] Spare yourself the
        trouble:
That hears he better from myself.
  Max. [*stepping backward.*] My Princess!
What have you let her hear me say, Aunt
        Tertsky?
  Thek. [*to the* Countess.] Has he been here
        long?
  Coun.   Yes; and soon must go.
Where have *you* stayed so long?
  Thek.   Alas! my mother
Wept so again! and I—I see her suffer,
Yet cannot keep myself from being happy.
  Max. Now once again I have courage to look
        on you.
To-day at noon I could not.
The dazzle of the jewels that played round you
Hid the beloved from me.
  Thek.   Then you saw me
With your eye only—and not with your heart?
  Max. This morning, when I found you in the
        circle
Of all your kindred, in your father's arms,

Beheld myself an alien in this circle,
O! what an impulse felt I in that moment
To fall upon his neck, and call him *father!*
But his stern eye o'erpower'd the swelling passion,
It dared not but be silent. And those brilliants,
That like a crown of stars enwreathed your brows,
They scared me too! O wherefore, wherefore should he
At the firs meeting spread as 'twere the ban
Of excommunication round you, wherefore
Dress up the angel as for sacrifice,
And cast upon the light and joyous heart
The mournful burthen of *his* station? Fitly
May love dare woo for love; but such a splendour
Might none but monarchs venture to approach.

Thek. Hush! not a word more of this mummery,
You see how soon the burthen is thrown off.
[*To the* Countess.] He is not in spirits. Wherefore is he not?
'Tis you, aunt, that have made him all so gloomy!
He had quite another nature on the journey—
So calm, so bright, so joyous, eloquent.
[*To* Max.] It was my wish to see you always so,
And never otherwise!

Max.   You find yourself
In your great father's arms, beloved lady!
All in a new world, which does homage to you,
And which, wer't only by its novelty,
Delights your eye.

Thek.   Yes; I confess to you
That many things delight me here: this camp,
This motley stage of warriors, which renews
So manifold the image of my fancy,
And binds to life, binds to reality,
What hitherto had but been present to me
As a sweet dream!
   Max.   Alas! not so to me,
It makes a dream of my reality.
Upon some island in the ethereal heights
I've lived for these last days. This mass of men
Forces me down to earth. It is a bridge
That, reconducting to my former life,
Divides me and my heaven.
   Thek.   The game of life
Looks cheerful, when one carries in one's heart
The inalienable treasure. 'Tis a game,
Which having once reviewed, I turn more joyous
Back to my deeper and appropriate bliss.
            [*Breaking off, and in a sportive tone.*
In this short time that I've been present here,
What new unheard-of things have I not seen!
And yet they all must give place to the wonder
Which this mysterious castle guards.
   Coun. [*recollecting.*]   And what
Can this be then? Methought I was acquainted
With all the dusky corners of this house.
   Thek. Ay, [*smiling,*] but the road thereto is
        watched by spirits.
Two griffins still stand sentry at the door.

Coun. [*laughs.*] The astrological tower!—
         How happens it
That this same sanctuary, whose access
Is to all others so impracticable,
Opens before you even at your approach?
  Thek. A dwarfish old man with a friendly face
And snow-white hairs, whose gracious services
Were mine at first sight, opened me the doors.
  Max. That is the Duke's astrologer, old Seni.
  Thek. He questioned me on many points; for
         instance,
When I was born, what month, and on what day,
Whether by day or in the night.
  Coun.   He wished
To erect a figure for your horoscope.
  Thek. My hand too he examined, shook his
         head
With such sad meaning, and the lines, methought,
Did not square over truly with his wishes.
  Coun. Well, Princess, and what found you in
         this tower?
My highest privilege has been to snatch
A side-glance, and away!
  Thek.   It was a strange
Sensation that came o'er me, when at first
From the broad sunshine I stept in; and now
The narrowing line of day-light, that ran after
The closing door, was gone; and all about me
'Twas pale and dusky night, with many shadows
Fantastically cast.   Here six or seven

Colossal statues, and all kings, stood round me
In a half-circle. Each one in his hand
A sceptre bore, and on his head a star;
And in the tower no other light was there
But from these stars: all seemed to come from
      them.
"These are the planets," said that low old man.
"They govern worldly fates, and for that cause
Are imaged here as kings. He farthest from you,
Spiteful, and cold, an old man melancholy,
With bent and yellow forehead, he is Saturn.
He opposite, the king with the red light,
An armed man for the battle, that is Mars:
And both these bring but little luck to man."
But at his side a lovely lady stood,
The star upon her head was soft and bright,
And that was Venus, the bright star of joy.
On the left hand, lo! Mercury, with wings.
Quite in the middle glittered silver bright
A cheerful man, and with a monarch's mien;
And this was Jupiter, my father's star:
And at his side I saw the Sun and Moon.

  Max. O never rudely will I blame his faith
In the might of stars and angels! 'Tis not merely
The human being's Pride that peoples space
With life and mystical predominance;
Since likewise for the stricken heart of Love
This visible nature, and this common world,
Is all too narrow: yea, a deeper import
Lurks in the legend told my infant years

Than lies upon that truth, we live to learn.
For fable is Love's world, his home, his birth-
    place:
Delightedly dwells he 'mong fays and talismans,
And spirits; and delightedly believes
Divinities, being himself divine.
The intelligible forms of ancient poets,
The fair humanities of old religion,
The power, the beauty, and the majesty,
That had their haunts in dale, or piny mountain,
Or forest by slow stream, or pebbly spring,
Or chasms and wat'ry depths; all these have
    vanished;
They live no longer in the faith of reason!
But still the heart doth need a language, still
Doth the old instinct bring back the old names,
And to yon starry world they now are gone,
Spirits or gods, that used to share this earth
With man as with their friend; and to the lover
Yonder they move, from yonder visible sky
Shoot influence down: and even at this day
'Tis Jupiter brings whate'er is great,
And Venus who brings everything that's fair!

  Thek. And if this be the science of the stars,
I too, with glad and zealous industry,
Will learn acquaintance with this cheerful faith.
It is a gentle and affectionate thought,
That in immeasurable heights above us,
At our first birth, the wreath of love was woven,
With sparkling stars for flowers.

Coun.   Not only roses,
But thorns too hath the heaven; and well for you
Leave they your wreath of love inviolate;
What Venus twined, the bearer of glad fortune,
The sullen orb of Mars soon tears to pieces.

  Max. Soon will his gloomy empire reach its
        close.
Blest be the general's zeal: into the laurel
Will he inweave the olive-branch, presenting
Peace to the shouting nations. Then no wish
Will have remained for his great heart! Enough
Has he performed for glory, and can now
Live for himself and his. To his domains
Will he retire; he has a stately seat
Of fairest view at Gitschin; Reichenberg,
And Friedland Castle, both lie pleasantly—
Even to the foot of the huge mountains here
Stretches the chase and covers of his forests:
His ruling passion, to create the splendid,
He can indulge without restraint; can give
A princely patronage to every art,
And to all worth a Sovereign's protection;
Can build, can plant, can watch the starry cour-
        ses—

  Coun. Yet I would have you look, and look
        again,
Before you lay aside your arms, young friend!
A gentle bride, as she is, is well worth it,
That you should woo and win her with the sword.

  Max. O, that the sword could win her!

Coun. What was that?
Did you hear nothing? Seemed, as if I heard
Tumult and larum in the banquet-room.

[*Exit* Countess.

Scene V.—Thekla *and* Max. Piccolomini.

Thek. [*as soon as the* Countess *is out of sight, in a quick low voice to* Piccolomini.] Don't trust them! They are false!

Max. Impossible!

Thek. Trust no one here but me. I saw at once,
They had a *purpose*.

Max. Purpose! but what purpose?
And how can we be instrumental to it?

Thek. I know no more than you; but yet believe me:
There's some design in this! to make us happy,
To realize our union—trust me, love!
They but pretend to wish it.

Max. But these Tertskys——
Why use we them at all? Why not your mother?
Excellent creature! she deserves from us
A full and filial confidence.

Thek. She doth love you,
Doth rate you high before all others—but—
But such a secret—she would never have
The courage to conceal it from my father.
For her own peace of mind we must preserve it
A secret from her too.

Max.   Why any secret?
I love not secrets. Mark, what I will do.
I'll throw me at your father's feet—let *him*
Decide upon my fortunes!—He is true,
He wears no mask—he hates all crooked ways—
He is so good, so noble!
   Thek. [*falls on his neck.*] *That* are you!
   Max. You knew him only since this morn;
          but I
Have lived ten years already in his presence,
And who knows whether in this very moment
He is not merely waiting for us both
To own our loves, in order to unite us.
You are silent!———
You look at me with such a hopelessness!
What have you to object against your father?
   Thek. I? Nothing. Only he's so occupied—
He has no leisure time to think about
The happiness of us two.   [*Taking his hand tenderly.*
           Follow me!
Let us not place too great a faith in men.
These Tertskys—we will still be grateful to them
For every kindness, but not trust them further
Than they deserve;—and in all else rely——
On our own hearts!
   Max.   O! shall we *e'er* be happy?
     Thek. Are we not happy now? Art thou not
         mine?
Am I not thine? There lives within my soul
A lofty courage—'tis love gives it me!

I ought to be less open—ought to hide
My heart more from thee—so decorum dictates:
But where in this place couldst thou seek for truth,
If in my mouth thou didst not find it?

Scene VI.—*To them enters the* Countess Tertsky.

Coun. [*in a pressing manner.*]　　　Come!
My husband sends me for you.—It is now
The latest moment. [*they not appearing to attend to what she says, she steps between them.*]
　　　　　　　Part you!
Thek.　　　　　　O, not yet!
It has been scarce a moment.
　Coun.　　　　　　Ay! Then time
Flies swiftly with your Highness, Princess niece!
　Max. There is no hurry, aunt.
　Coun.　　　　　　Away! away!
The folks begin to miss you. Twice already
His father has asked for him.
　Thek.　　　　　　Ha! his father?
　Coun. You understand *that*, niece!
　Thek.　　　　　　Why needs he
To go at all to that society?
'Tis not his proper company. They may
Be worthy men, but he's too young for them.
In brief, he suits not such society.
　Coun. You mean, you'd rather keep him wholly here?

Thek. [*with energy.*] Yes! you have hit it, aunt! That is my meaning.
Leave him here wholly! Tell the company—
  Coun. What? have you lost your senses, niece?—
Count, you remember the conditions. Come!
  Max. [*to* THEKLA.] Lady, I must obey. Farewell, dear lady!

  [THEKLA *turns away from him with a quick motion.*
What say you then, dear lady?
  Thek. [*without looking at him.*] Nothing. Go!
  Max. Can I, when you are angry——

  [*He draws up to her, their eyes meet, she stands silent a moment, then throws herself into his arms; he presses her fast to his heart.*

Coun. Off! Heavens! if any one should come! Hark! What's that noise? It comes this way.—— Off!

  [MAX. *tears himself away out of her arms, and goes. The* COUNTESS *accompanies him.* THEKLA *follows him with her eyes at first, walks restlessly across the room, then stops, and remains standing, lost in thought. A guitar lies on the table, she seizes it as by a sudden emotion, and after she has played awhile an irregular and melancholy symphony, she falls gradually into the music and sings.*

Thekla (*plays and sings*).

The cloud doth gather, the greenwood roar,
The damsel paces along the shore;
The billows they tumble with might, with might;
And she flings out her voice to the darksome night;

Her bosom is swelling with sorrow;
The world it is empty, the heart will die,
There's nothing to wish for beneath the sky:
Thou Holy One, call thy child away!
I've lived and loved, and that was to-day—
  Make ready my grave-clothes to-morrow.*

---

* I found it not in my power to translate this song with *literal* fidelity, preserving at the same time the Alcaic movement; and have therefore added the original with a prose translation. Some of my readers may be more fortunate.

THEKLA (*spielt und singt.*)

Der Eichwald brauset, die Wolken ziehn,
Das Mägdlein wandelt an Ufers Grün,
Es bricht sich die Welle mit Macht, mit Macht,
Und sie singt hinaus in die finstre Nacht,
  Das Auge von Weinen getrübet:
Das Herz ist gestorben, die Welt ist leer,
Und weiter giebt sie dem Wunsche nichts mehr.
Du Heilige, rufe dein Kind zurück,
Ich habe genossen das irdische Glück,
  Ich habe gelebt und geliebet.

Literal Translation.

THEKLA (*plays and sings.*)

The oak-forest bellows, the clouds gather, the damsel walks to and fro on the green of the shore; the wave breaks with might, with might, and she sings out into the dark night, her eye discoloured with weeping: the heart is dead, the world is empty, and further gives it nothing more to the wish. Thou Holy One, call thy child home. I have enjoyed the happiness of this world, I have lived and have loved.

I cannot but add here an imitation of this song, with which the author of "The Tale of Rosamund Gray and Blind Margaret" has favoured me, and which appears to me to have caught the happiest manner of our old ballads.

Scene VII.—Countess (*returns*,) Thekla.

Coun. Fie, lady niece! to throw yourself upon him,
Like a poor gift to one who cares not for it,
And so must be flung after him! For you,
Duke Friedland's only child, I should have thought,
It had been more beseeming to have shown yourself
More chary of your person.
Thek. [*rising.*]   And what mean you?
Coun. I mean, niece, that you should not have forgotten
Who *you* are, and who he is. But perchance
That never once occurred to you.
Thek.   What then?
Coun. That you are the daughter of the Prince Duke Friedland.
Thek. Well—and what farther?
Coun.   What? a pretty question!
Thek. He was *born* that which we have but *become*.

The clouds are blackening, the storms threatening,
  The cavern doth mutter, the greenwood moan;
Billows are breaking, the damsel's heart aching,
  Thus in the dark night she singeth alone,
    Her eye upward roving:
The world is empty, the heart is dead surely,
  In this world plainly all seemeth amiss;
To thy heaven, Holy One, take home thy little one,
  I have partaken of all earth's bliss,
    Both living and loving.

He's of an ancient Lombard family,
Son of a reigning princess.
 Coun.   Are you dreaming?
Talking in sleep? An excellent jest, forsooth!
We shall no doubt right courteously *entreat*
  him
To honour with his hand the richest heiress
In Europe.
 Thek. That will not be necessary.
 Coun. Methinks 'twere well though not to run
  the hazard.
 Thek. His father loves him, Count Octavio
Will interpose no difficulty——
 Coun.   *His!*
His father! *his!* But yours, niece, what of
  yours?
 Thek. Why I begin to think you fear his father.
So anxiously you hide it from the man!
His father, *his*, I mean.
 Coun. [*looks at her as scrutinizing.*] Niece, you
  are *false*.
 Thek. Are you then wounded? O, be friends
  with me!
 Coun. You hold your game for one already.
  Do not
Triumph too soon!—
 Thek. [*interrupting her, and attempting to soothe
  her.*] [Nay now, be friends with me.
 Coun. It is not yet so far gone.
 Thek.   I believe you.

Coun. Did you suppose your father had laid out
His most important life in toils of war,
Denied himself each quiet earthly bliss,
Had banished slumber from his tent, devoted
His noble head to care, and for this only,
To make a happy pair of you? At length
To draw you from your convent, and conduct
In easy triumph to yours arms the man
That chanced to please your eyes! All this, me-
    thinks,
He might have purchased at a cheaper rate.
  Thek. That which he did not plant for me might
    yet
Bear me fair fruitage of its own accord.
And if my friendly and affectionate fate,
Out of his fearful and enormous being,
Will but prepare the joys of life for me—
  Coun. Thou seest it with a lovelorn maiden's
    eyes.
Cast thine eye round, bethink thee who thou art.
Into no house of joyance hast thou stepped,
For no espousals dost thou find the walls
Decked out, no guests the nuptial garland wearing.
Here is no splendour but of arms. Or think'st
    thou
That all these thousands are here congregated
To lead up the long dances at thy wedding?
Thou seest thy father's forehead full of thought,
Thy mother's eye in tears: upon the balance
Lies the great destiny of all our house.

Leave now the puny wish, the girlish feeling,
O thrust it far behind thee! Give thou proof,
Thou'rt the daughter of the Mighty—*his*
Who where he moves creates the wonderful.
Not to herself the woman must belong,
Annexed and bound to alien destinies.
But she performs the best part, she the wisest,
Who can transmute the alien into self;
Meet and disarm necessity by choice,
And what must be, take freely to her heart,
And bear and foster it with mother's love.

 Thek. Such ever was my lesson in the convent.
I had no loves, no wishes, knew myself
Only as his—daughter—his, the Mighty!
His fame, the echo of whose blast drove to me
From the far distance, wakened in my soul
No other thought than this—I am appointed
To offer up myself in passiveness to him.

 Coun. That *is* thy fate. Mould thou thy wishes
  to it.
I and thy mother gave thee the example.

 Thek. My fate hath shown me *him,* to whom be-
  hoves it
That I should offer up myself. In gladness
Him will I follow.

 Coun.   Not thy fate hath shown him!
Thy heart, say rather—'twas thy heart, my child!

 Thek. Fate hath no voice but the heart's im-
  pulses.
I am all *his!* *His* present—his alone,

Is this new life, which lives in me. He hath
A right to his own creature. What was I
Ere his fair love infused a soul into me?

   Coun. Thou wouldst oppose thy father then, should he
Have otherwise determined with thy person?

   [THEKLA *remains silent. The* COUNTESS *continues.*
Thou mean'st to force him to thy liking?—Child,
His name is Friedland.

   Thek.   *My* name too is Friedland.
He shall have found a genuine daughter in me.

   Coun. What? he has vanquished all impediment,
And in the wilful mood of his own daughter
Shall a new struggle rise for him? Child! child!
As yet thou hast seen thy father's smiles alone;
The eye of his rage thou hast not seen. Dear child,
I will not frighten thee. To that extreme,
I trust, it ne'er shall come. His will is yet
Unknown to me: 'tis possible his aims
May have the same direction as thy wish.
But this can never, never be his will
That thou, the daughter of his haughty fortunes,
Should'st e'er demean thee as a lovesick maiden;
And like some poor cost-nothing, fling thyself
Toward the man, who, *if* that high prize ever
Be destined to await him, yet, with sacrifices
The highest love can bring, must pay for it.
                       [*Exit* COUNTESS.

Thek. [*who during the last speech had been lost in her reflections.*] I thank thee for the hint. It turns
My sad presentiment to certainty.
And it is so!—Not one friend have we here,
Not one true heart! we've nothing but ourselves!
O she said rightly—no auspicious signs
Beam on this covenant of our affections.
This is no theatre, where hope abides.
The dull thick noise of war alone stirs here.
And love himself, as he were armed in steel,
Steps forth, and girds him for the strife of death.

[*Music from the banquet-room is heard.*

There's a dark spirit walking in our house,
And swiftly will the Destiny close on us.
It drove me hither from my calm asylum,
It mocks my soul with charming witchery,
It lures me forward in a seraph's shape,
I see it near, I see it nearer floating,
It draws, it pulls me with a god-like power—
And lo! the abyss—and thither am I moving—
I have no power within me not to move!

[*The music from the banquet-room becomes louder.*

O when a house is doomed in fire to perish,
Many a dark heaven drives his clouds together,
Yea, shoots his lightnings down from sunny heights,
Flames burst from out the subterraneous chasms,

*And fiends and angels mingling in their fury,
Sling firebrands at the burning edifice.
                              [*Exit* THEKLA.

SCENE VIII.—*A large Saloon lighted up with festal splendour; in the midst of it, and in the centre of the Stage, a Table richly set out, at which eight* Generals *are sitting, among whom are* OCTAVIO PICCOLOMINI, TERTSKY, *and* MARADAS. *Right and left of this, but farther back, two other Tables, at each of which six Persons are placed. The Middle Door, which is standing open, gives to the Prospect a fourth Table, with the same number of Persons. More forward stands the Sideboard. The whole front of the Stage is kept open for the* Pages *and* Servants *in waiting. All is in motion. The band of Music belonging to* TERTSKY'S *Regiment march across the Stage, and draw up round the Tables. Before they are quite off from the Front of the Stage,* MAX. PICCOLOMINI *appears,* TERTSKY *advances towards him with a Paper,* ISOLANI *comes up to meet him with a Beaker or Service-cup.*

TERTSKY, ISOLANI, MAX. PICCOLOMINI.

Iso. Here, brother, what we love! Why, where
        hast been?
Off to thy place—quick! Tertsky here has given
The mother's holiday wine up to free booty.

---

* There are few who will not have taste enough to laugh at the two concluding lines of this soliloquy; and still fewer, I would fain hope, who would not have been more disposed to shudder, had I given a faithful translation. For the readers of German I have added the original:

Blind-wüthend schleudert selbst der Gott der Freude
Den Pechkranz in das brennende Gebäude.

Here it goes on as at the Heidelberg castle.
Already hast thou lost the best. They're giving
At yonder table ducal crowns in shares;
There's Sternberg's lands and chattels are put up,
With Egenberg's, Stawata's, Lichtenstein's,
And all the great Bohemian feodalities.
Be nimble, lad! and something may turn up
For thee—who knows? off—to thy place! quick!
    march!

Tiefenbach and Goetz. [*call out from the second and third tables.*] Count Piccolomini!

Ter. Stop, ye shall have him in an instant.—
    Read
This oath here, whether as 'tis here set forth,
The wording satisfies you. They've all read it,
Each in his turn, and each one will subscribe
His individual signature.

Max. [*reads.*] "Ingratis servire nefas."

Iso. That sounds to my ears very much like
    Latin,
And being interpreted, pray what may't mean?

Ter. No honest man will serve a thankless
    master.

Max. "Inasmuch as our supreme Commander, the illustrious Duke of Friedland, in consequence of the manifold affronts and grievances which he has received, has expressed his determination to quit the Emperor, but on our unanimous entreaty has graciously consented to remain still with the army, and not to part from us without our approbation thereof, so we, collectively and *each in particular*, in the stead of an oath personally taken, do hereby oblige ourselves—likewise by him honourably and faithfully to hold, and in nowise whatsoever from him to part, and to be ready to shed for his interests the last drop of our blood, so far, namely, as *our oath to the Emperor will permit it.* [*These last words are repeated by* ISOLANI.] In testimony of which we subscribe our names."

Ter. Now!—are you willing to subscribe this
    paper?

Iso. Why should he not? All officers of honour
Can do it, ay, must do it.—Pen and ink here!

Ter. Nay, let it rest till after meal.

Iso. [*drawing Max. along.*]   Come Max.
        [*Both seat themselves at their table.*

SCENE IX.—TERTSKY, NEUMANN.

Ter. [*beckons to* NEUMANN, *who is waiting at the side-table, and steps forward with him to the edge of the stage.*] Have you the copy with you,
    Neumann? Give it.
It may be changed for the other?

Neu.   I have copied it
Letter by letter, line by line; no eye
Would e'er discover other difference,
Save only the omission of that clause,
According to your Excellency's order.

Ter. Right! lay it yonder, and away with this—
It has performed its business—to the fire with it—
 [NEUMANN *lays the copy on the table, and steps back
  again to the side table.*

SCENE X.—ILLO (*comes out from the second chamber,*)
 TERTSKY.

Illo. How goes it with young Piccolomini?
Ter. All right, I think. He has started no
  objection.
Illo. He is the only one I fear about—
He and his father. Have an eye on both!
Ter. How looks it at your table: you forget not
To keep them warm and stirring?
Illo.   O, quite cordial,
They are quite cordial in the scheme. We have
  them.
And 'tis as I predicted, too. Already
It is the talk, not merely to maintain
The Duke in station. "Since we're once for all
Together and unanimous, why not,"
Says Montecuculi, "ay, why not onward,
And make conditions with the Emperor
There in his own Vienna?" Trust me, Count,
Were it not for these said Piccolomini,
We might have spared ourselves the cheat.
   Ter.   And Butler?
How goes it there? Hush!

SCENE XI.—*To them enter* BUTLER *from the second table.*

But. Don't disturb yourselves.
Field Marshal, I have understood you perfectly.
Good luck be to the scheme; and as to me,
   [*With an air of mystery.*
You may depend upon me.
 Illo. [*with vivacity.*] May we, Butler?
 But. With or without the clause, all one to me!
You understand me? My fidelity
The Duke may put to any proof—I'm with him!
Tell him so! I'm the Emperor's officer,
As long as 'tis his pleasure to remain
The Emperor's general! and Friedland's servant,
As soon as it shall please him to become
His own lord.
 Ter. You would make a good exchange.
No stern economist, no Ferdinand,
Is he to whom you plight your services.
 But. [*with a haughty look.*] I do not put up my
    fidelity
To sale, Count Tertsky! Half a year ago
I would not have advised you to have made me
An overture to that, to which I now
Offer myself of my own free accord.—
But that is past! and to the Duke, Field Marshal,
I bring myself together with my regiment.
And mark you, 'tis my humour to believe,
The example which I give will not remain
Without an influence.
 Illo. Who is ignorant,

That the whole army look to Colonel Butler,
As to a light that moves before them?
 But.   Ey?
Then I repent me not of that fidelity
Which for the length of forty years I held,
If in my sixtieth year my old good name
Can purchase for me a revenge so full.
Start not at what I say, sir Generals!
My real motives—they concern not you.
And you yourselves, I trust, could not expect
That this your game had crooked *my* judgment—or
That fickleness, quick blood, or such light cause,
Had driven the old man from the track of honour,
Which he so long had trodden.—Come, my friends!
I'm not thereto determined with less firmness,
Because I know and have looked steadily
At that on which I have determined.
 Illo.   Say,
And speak roundly, what are we to deem you?
 But. A friend! I give you here my hand! I'm
   yours
With all I have. Not only men, but money
Will the Duke want.——Go, tell him, sirs!
I've earned and laid up somewhat in his service,
I lend it him; and is he my survivor,
It has been already long ago bequeathed him.
He is my heir. For me, I stand alone,
Here in the world; nought know I of the feeling
That binds the husband to a wife and children.
My name dies with me, my existence ends.

Illo. 'Tis not your money that he needs—a heart
Like yours weighs tons of gold down, weighs down
      millions!

But. I came a simple soldier's boy from Ireland
To Prague—and with a master, whom I buried.
From lowest stable duty I climbed up,
Such was the fate of war, to this high rank,
The plaything of a whimsical good fortune.
And Wallenstein too is a child of luck,
I love a fortune that is like my own.

Illo. All powerful souls have kindred with each
      other.

But. This is an awful moment! to the brave,
To the determined, an auspicious moment.
The Prince of Weimar arms, upon the Maine
To found a mighty dukedom. He of Halberstadt,
That Mansfeld, wanted but a longer life
To have marked out with his good sword a lord-
      ship
That should reward his courage. Who of these
Equals our Friedland? There is nothing, nothing
So high, but he may set the ladder to it!

Ter. That's spoken like a man!

But. Do you secure the Spaniard and Italian—
I'll be your warrant for the Scotchman Lesly.
Come! to the company!

Ter. Where is the master of the cellar? Ho!
Let the best wines come up. Ho! cheerly, boy!
Luck comes to-day, so give her hearty welcome.
              [*Exeunt, each to his table.*

Scene XII.—*The* Master of the Cellar *advancing with* Neumann, Servants *passing backwards and forwards.*

Mast. of the Cel. The best wine! O! if my old mistress, his lady mother, could but see these wild goings on, she would turn herself round in her grave. Yes, yes, sir officer! 'tis all down the hill with this noble house! no end, no moderation! And this marriage with the Duke's sister, a splendid connection, a very splendid connection! but I tell you, sir officer, it bodes no good.

Neu. Heaven forbid! Why, at this very moment the whole prospect is in bud and blossom!

Mast. of the Cel. You think so?—Well, well! much may be said on that head.

1st. Ser. [*comes.*] Burgundy for the fourth table.

Mast. of the Cel. Now, sir lieutenant, if this isn't the seventieth flask——

1st. Ser. Why, the reason is, that German lord, Tiefenbach, sits at that table.

Mast. of the Cel. [*continuing his discourse to* Neumann.] They are soaring too high. They would rival kings and electors in their pomp and splendour; and wherever the Duke leaps, not a minute does my gracious master, the Count, loiter on the brink.——[*to the* Servants.]—What do you stand there listening for? I will let you know you have legs presently. Off! see to the tables, see to the flasks! Look there! Count Palfi has an empty glass before him!

Runner. [*comes.*] The great service-cup is wanted, sir; that rich gold cup with the Bohemian arms on it. The Count says you know which it is.

Mast. of the Cel. Ay! that was made for Frederick's coronation by the artist William—there was not such another prize in the whole booty at Prague.

Runner. The same!—a health is to go round in him.

Mast. of the Cel. [*shaking his head, while he fetches and rinses the cup.*] This will be something for the tale-bearers—this goes to Vienna.

Neu. Permit me to look at it.—Well, this is a cup indeed! How heavy! as well it may be, being all gold.—And what neat things are embossed on it! how natural and elegant they look! There on that first quarter, let me see. That proud Amazon there on horseback, she that is taking a leap over the crosier and mitres, and carries on a wand a hat together with a banner, on which there's a goblet represented. Can you tell me what all this signifies?

Mast of the Cel. The woman whom you see there on horseback, is the Free Election of the Bohemian Crown. That is signified by the round hat, and by that fiery steed on which she is riding. The hat is the pride of man; for he who cannot keep his hat on before kings and emperors is no free man.

Neu. But what is the cup there on the banner?

Mast. of the Cel. The cup signifies the freedom of the Bohemian Church, as it was in our forefathers' times. Our forefathers in the wars of the Hussites forced from the Pope this noble privilege: for the Pope, you know, will not grant the cup to any layman. Your true Moravian values nothing beyond the cup; it is his costly jewel, and has cost the Bohemians their precious blood in many and many a battle.

Neu. And what says that chart that hangs in the air there, over it all?

Mast. of the Cel. That signifies the Bohemian letter royal, which we forced from the Emperor Rudolph—a precious, never-to-be-enough valued parchment, that secures to the new Church the old privileges of free ringing and open psalmody. But since he of Steiermärk has ruled over us, that is at an end; and after the battle at Prague, in which Count Palatine Frederick lost crown and empire, our faith hangs upon the pulpit and the altar—and our brethren look at their homes over their shoulders; but the letter royal the Emperor himself cut to pieces with his scissors.

Neu. Why, my good Master of the Cellar! you are deep read in the chronicles of your country!

Mast. of the Cel. So were my forefathers, and for that reason were they minstrels, and served under Procopius and Ziska. Peace be with their ashes! Well, well! they fought for a good cause though—There! carry it up!

Neu. Stay! let me but look at this second quarter. Look *there!* That is, when at Prague Castle the Imperial Counsellors, Martinitz and Stawata, were hurled down head over heels. 'Tis even so! there stands Count Thur who commands it.

[Runner *takes the service-cup and goes off with it.*

Mast. of the Cel. O let me never more hear of that day. It was the three-and-twentieth of May, in the year of our Lord one thousand, six hundred, and eighteen. It seems to me as it were but yesterday—from that unlucky day it all began, all the heart-aches of the country. Since that day it is now sixteen years, and there has never once been peace on the earth.

[*Health drunk aloud at the second table.*

The Prince of Weimar! Hurra!

[*At the third and fourth table.*

Long live Prince William! Long live Duke Bernard! Hurra! [*Music strikes up.*

1st Ser. Hear 'em! Hear 'em! What an uproar!

2nd Ser. [*comes in running.*] Did you hear? They have drunk the Prince of Weimar's health.

3rd Ser. The Swedish Chief Commander!

1st Ser. [*speaking at the same time.*] The Lutheran!

2nd Ser. Just before when Count Deodate gave out the Emperor's health, they were all as mum as a nibbling mouse.

Mast. of the Cel. Poh, poh! When the wine

goes in, strange things come out. A good servant hears, and hears not!—You should be nothing but eyes and feet, except when you are called.

2nd Ser. [*to the* Runner, *to whom he gives secretly a flask of wine, keeping his eye on the* Master of the Cellar, *standing between him and the* Runner.] Quick, Thomas! before the Master of the Cellar runs this way!—'tis a flask of Frontignac!—Snapped it up at the third table.—Canst go off with it?

Run. [*hides it in his pocket.*] All right!

[*Exit the Second* Servant.

3rd Ser. [*aside to the First.*] Be on the hark, Jack! that we may have right plenty to tell to Father Quivoga—He will give us right plenty of absolution in return for it.

1st Ser. For that very purpose I am always having something to do behind Illo's chair.—He is the man for speeches to make you stare with!

Mast. of the Cel. [*to* NEUMANN.] Who, pray, may that swarthy man be, he with the cross, that is chatting so confidentially with Esterhats?

Neu. Ay! he too is one of those to whom they confide too much. He calls himself Maradas, a Spaniard is he.

Mast. of the Cel. [*impatiently.*] Spaniard! Spaniard!—I tell you, friend; nothing good comes of those Spaniards. All these outlandish* fellows are little better than rogues.

* There is a humour in the original which cannot be given

Neu. Fy, fy! you should not say so, friend. There are among them our very best generals, and those on whom the Duke at this moment relies the most.

Mast. of the Cell. [*taking the flask out of the* Runner's *pocket.*] My son, it will be broken to pieces in your pocket.

[TERTSKY *hurries in, fetches away the paper, and calls to a* Servant *for pen and ink, and goes to the back of the stage.*

Mast. of the Cel. [*to the* Servants.] The Lieutenant-General stands up.—Be on the watch.—Now! They break up.—Off, and move back the forms.

[*They rise at all the tables; the* Servants *hurry off the front of the stage to the tables; part of the* Guests *come forward.*

SCENE XIII.—OCTAVIO PICCOLOMINI *enters in conversation with* MARADAS, *and both place themselves quite on the edge of the stage on one side of the proscenium. On the side directly opposite,* MAX. PICCOLOMINI, *by himself, lost in thought, and taking no part in any thing that is going forward. The middle space between both, but rather more distant from the edge of the stage, is filled up by* BUTLER, ISOLANI, GOETZ, TIEFENBACH, *and* KOLATTO.

---

in the translation. "Die *welschen* alle," &c. which word in classical German means the *Italians* alone; but in its first sense, and at present in the *vulgar* use of the word, signifies foreigners in general. Our word wall-nuts, I suppose, means *outlandish* nuts—Wallæ nuces, in German "Welsch-nüsse."

Iso. [*while the company is coming forward.*] Good night, good night, Kolatto! Good night, Lieutenant-General!—I should rather say, good morning.

Goetz. [*to* TIEFENBACH, *making the usual compliment after meals.*] Noble brother!

Tief. Ay! 'twas a royal feast indeed.

Goetz. Yes, my Lady Countess understands these matters. Her mother-in-law, heaven rest her soul, taught her!—Ah! that was a housewife for you!

Tief. There was not her like in all Bohemia for setting out a table.

Oct. [*aside to* MARADAS.] Do me the favour to talk to me—talk of what you will—or of nothing. Only preserve the appearance at least of talking. I would not wish to stand by myself, and yet I conjecture that there will be goings on here worthy of our attentive observation.

[*He continues to fix his eye on the whole following scene.*

Iso. [*on the point of going.*] Lights! lights!

Ter. [*advances with the paper to* ISOLANI.] Noble brother! two minutes longer!—Here is something to subscribe.

Iso. Subscribe as much as you like—but you must excuse me from reading it.

Ter. There is no need. It is the oath which you have already read.—Only a few marks of your pen!

[ISOLANI *hands over the paper to* OCTAVIO *respectfully.*

Ter. Nay, nay, first come first served. There is no precedence here.

[OCTAVIO *runs over the paper with apparent indifference.* TERTSKY *watches him at some distance.*]

Goetz. [*to* TERTSKY.] Noble Count! with your permission—Good night.

Ter. Where's the hurry? Come, one other composing draught. [*To the* Servants.]—Ho!

Goetz. Excuse me—an't able.

Ter. A thimble-full!

Goetz. Excuse me.

Tief. [*sits down.*] Pardon me, nobles!—This standing does not agree with me.

Ter. Consult only your own convenience, General!

Tief. Clear at head, sound in stomach—only my legs won't carry me any longer.

Iso. [*pointing at his corpulence.*] Poor legs! how *should* they? Such an unmerciful load!

[OCTAVIO *subscribes his name, and reaches over the paper to* TERTSKY, *who gives it to* ISOLANI; *and he goes to the table to sign his name.*]

Tief. 'Twas that war in Pomerania that first brought it on. Out in all weathers—ice and snow—no help for it.—I shall never get the better of it all the days of my life.

Goetz. Why, in simple verity, your Swede makes no nice inquiries about the season.

Ter. [*observing* ISOLANI, *whose hand trembles excessively, so that he can scarce direct his pen.*]

Have you had that ugly complaint long, noble brother?—Dispatch it.

Iso. The sins of youth! I have already tried the Chalybeate waters. Well—I must bear it.

[TERTSKY *gives the paper to* MARADAS; *he steps to the table to subscribe.*

Oct. [*advancing to* BUTLER.] You are not over fond of the orgies of Bacchus, Colonel! I have observed it. You would, I think, find yourself more to your liking in the uproar of a battle, than of a feast.

But. I must confess, 'tis not in my way.

Oct. [*stepping nearer to him, friendlily.*] Nor in mine either, I can assure you; and I am not a little glad, my much honoured Colonel Butler, that we agree so well in our opinions. A half dozen good friends at most, at a small round table, a glass of genuine Tokay, open hearts, and a rational conversation—that's my taste!

But. And mine too, when it can be had.

[*The paper comes to* TIEFENBACH, *who glances over it at the same time with* GOETZ *and* KOLATTO. MARADAS *in the mean time returns to* OCTAVIO; *all this takes place, the conversation with* BUTLER *proceeding uninterrupted.*

Oct. [*introducing* MARADAS *to* BUTLER.] Don Balthasar Maradas! likewise a man of our stamp, and long ago your admirer. [BUTLER *bows.*

Oct. [*continuing.*] You are a stranger here— 'twas but yesterday you arrived—you are ignorant of the ways and means here. 'Tis a wretched place—I know, at our age, one loves to be snug and quiet—What if you moved your lodgings?—Come, be my visitor. [BUTLER *makes a low bow.*] Nay, without compliment!—For a friend like you, I have still a corner remaining.

But. [*coldly.*] Your obliged humble servant, My Lord Lieutenant-General!

> [*The paper comes to* BUTLER, *who goes to the table to subscribe it. The front of the stage is vacant, so that both the* PICCOLOMINIS, *each on the side where he had been from the commencement of the scene, remain alone.*]

Oct. [*after having some time watched his son in silence, advances somewhat nearer to him.*] You were long absent from us, friend!

Max. I——urgent business detained me.

Oct. And, I observe, you are still absent!

Max. You know this crowd and bustle always makes me silent.

Oct. May I be permitted to ask what business 'twas that detained you? *Tertsky* knows it without asking!

Max. What does Tertsky know?

Oct. He was the only one who did not miss you.

Iso. [*who has been attending to them from some distance, steps up.*] Well done, father! Rout out his baggage! Beat up his quarters! there is something there that should not be.

Ter. [*with the paper.*] Is there none wanting? Have the whole subscribed?

Oct. All.

Ter. [*calling aloud.*] Ho! Who subscribes?

But. [*to* TERTSKY.] Count the names. There ought to be just thirty.

Ter. Here is a cross.

Tief. That's my mark.

Iso. He cannot write; but his cross is a good cross, and is honoured by Jews as well as Christians.

Oct. [*presses on to* MAX.] Come, General! let us go. It is late.

Ter. One Piccolomini only has signed.

Iso. [*pointing to* MAX.] Look! that is your man, that statue there, who has had neither eye, ear, nor tongue for us the whole evening.

[MAX. *receives the paper from* TERTSKY, *which he looks upon vacantly.*

SCENE XIV.—*To these enter* ILLO *from the inner room. He has in his hand the golden service-cup, and is extremely distempered with drinking;* GOETZ *and* BUTLER *follow him, endeavouring to keep him back.*

Illo. What do you want? Let me go.

Goetz and But. Drink no more, Illo! For heaven's sake drink no more.

Illo. [*goes up to* OCTAVIO *and shakes him cordially by the hand, and then drinks.*] Octavio! I bring this to you. Let all grudge be drowned in this friendly bowl! I know well enough, ye never loved me—Devil take me!—and I never loved you!—I am always even with people in that way!—Let what's past be past—that is, you understand—forgotten! I esteem you infinitely. [*Embracing him repeatedly.*] You have not a dearer friend on earth than I—but that you know. The fellow that cries rogue to you calls me villain—and I'll strangle him!—my *dear* friend!

Ter. [*whispering to him.*] Art in thy senses? For heaven's sake, Illo! think where you are!

Illo. [*aloud.*] What do you mean?—There are none but friends here, are there? [*Looks round the whole circle with a jolly and triumphant air.*] Not a sneaker among us, thank heaven!

Ter. [*to* BUTLER, *eagerly.*] Take him off with you, force him off, I entreat you, Butler!

But. [*to* ILLO.] Field Marshal! a word with you! [*Leads him to the side-board.*

Illo. A thousand for one; Fill—fill it once more up to the brim.—To this gallant man's health!

Iso. [*to* MAX. *who all the while has been staring on the paper with fixed but vacant eyes.*] Slow and sure, my noble brother?—Hast *parsed* it all yet?—Some words yet to go through?—Ha?

Max. [*waking up as from a dream.*] What am I to do?

Ter. [*and at the same time* ISOLANI.] Sign your name.

[OCTAVIO *directs his eyes on him with intense anxiety.*

Max. [*returns the paper.*] Let it stay till to-morrow. It is business—to-day I am not sufficiently collected. Send it to me to-morrow.

Ter. Nay, collect yourself a little.

Iso. Awake, man! awake!—Come, thy signature, and have done with it! What? Thou art the youngest in the whole company, and wouldest be wiser than all of us together? Look there! thy father has signed—we have all signed.

Ter. [*to* OCTAVIO.] Use your influence. Instruct him.

Oct. My son is at the age of discretion.

Illo. [*leaves the service-cup on the side-board.*] What's the dispute?

Ter. He declines subscribing the paper.

Max. I say, it may as well stay till to-morrow.

Illo. It cannot stay. We have all subscribed to it—and so must you.—You must subscribe.

Max. Illo; good night!

Illo. No! You come not off so! The Duke shall learn who are his friends.

[*All collect round* ILLO *and* MAX.

Max. What my sentiments are towards the Duke the Duke knows, every one knows—what need of this wild stuff?

Illo. This is the thanks the Duke gets for his partiality to Italians and foreigners.—Us Bohemians he holds for little better than dullards— nothing pleases him but what's outlandish.

Ter. [*in extreme embarrassment, to the* Commanders, *who at* ILLO'S *words give a sudden start, as preparing to resent them.*] It is the wine that speaks, and not his reason. Attend not to him, I entreat you.

Iso. [*with a bitter laugh.*] Wine invents nothing: it only *tattles.*

Illo. He who is not with me, is against me. Your tender consciences! Unless they can slip out by a back-door, by a puny proviso——

Ter. [*interrupting him.*] He is stark mad—don't listen to him!

Illo. [*raising his voice to the highest pitch.*] Unless they can slip out by a *proviso.* What of the proviso? The devil take this proviso!

Max. [*has his attention roused and looks again into the paper.*] What is there here then of such perilous import? You make me curious—I must look closer at it.

Ter. [*in a low voice to* ILLO.] What are you doing, Illo? You are ruining us.

Tief. [*to* KOLATTO.] Ay, ay! I observed, that before we sat down to supper, it was read differently.

Goetz. Why, I seemed to think so too.

Iso. What do I care for that? Where there stand other names, mine can stand too.

Tief. Before supper there *was* a certain proviso therein, or short clause concerning our duties to the Emperor.

But. [*to one of the* Commanders.] For shame, for shame! Bethink you. What is the main business here? The question now is, whether we shall keep our General, or let him retire. One must not take these things too nicely and over-scrupulously.

Iso. [*to one of the* Generals.] Did the Duke make any of these provisos when he gave you your regiment?

Ter. [*to* Goetz.] Or when he gave you the office of army purveyancer, which brings you in yearly a thousand pistoles!

Illo. He is a rascal who makes us out to be rogues. If there be any one that wants satisfaction, let him say so, I am his man.

Tief. Softly, softly! 'Twas but a word or two.

Max. [*having read the paper gives it back.*] Till to-morrow, therefore!

Illo. [*stammering with rage and fury, loses all command over himself, and presents the paper to* Max. *with one hand, and his sword in the other.*] Subscribe—Judas!

Iso. Out upon you, Illo!

Oct. Ter. But. [*all together.*] Down with the sword!

Max. [*rushes on him suddenly and disarms him, then to* Count Tertsky.] Take him off to bed.

> [Max. *leaves the stage.* Illo *cursing and raving is held back by some of the officers, and amidst a universal confusion the curtain drops.*

ACT III.

Scene I.—*A Chamber in* Piccolomini's *Mansion. It is Night.* Octavio Piccolomini. *A* Valet de Chambre, *with Lights.*

Oct. ——And when my son comes in conduct
    him hither.
What is the hour?
    Valet.   'Tis on the point of morning.
    Oct. Set down the light. We mean not to
    undress.
You may retire to sleep.

[*Exit* Valet. Octavio *paces, musing, across the Chamber.* Max. Piccolomini *enters unobserved, and looks at his father for some moments in silence.*

    Max. Art *thou* offended with me? Heaven
    knows
That odious business was no fault of mine.
'Tis true, indeed, I saw thy signature.
What thou hadst sanctioned, should not, it might
    seem,
Have come amiss to me. But—'tis my nature—
Thou know'st that in such matters I must follow
My own light, not another's.
    Oct. [*goes up to him and embraces him.*] Follow it,

O follow it still further, my best son!
To-night, dear boy! it hath more faithfully
Guided thee than the example of thy father.

   Max. Declare thyself less darkly.

   Oct.   I will do so,
For after what has taken place this night,
There must remain no secrets 'twixt us two.
                                [*Both seat themselves.*

Max. Piccolomini! what think'st thou of
The oath that was sent round for signatures?

   Max. I hold it for a thing of harmless import,
Although I love not these set declarations.

   Oct. And on no other ground hast thou refused
The signature they fain had wrested from thee?

   Max. It was a serious business——I was absent—
The affair itself seemed not so urgent to me.

   Oct. Be open, Max. Thou hadst then no suspicion?

   Max. Suspicion! what suspicion? Not the least.

   Oct. Thank thy good angel, Piccolomini:
He drew thee back unconscious from the abyss.

   Max. I know not what thou meanest.

   Oct.   I will tell thee.
Fain would they have extorted from thee, son,
The sanction of thy name to villany;
Yea, with a single flourish of thy pen,
Made thee renounce thy duty and thy honour!

   Max. [*rises.*] Octavio!

Oct.   Patience! Seat yourself.   Much yet
Hast thou to hear from me, friend!—hast for years
Lived in incomprehensible illusion.
Before thine eyes is treason drawing out
As black a web as e'er was spun for venom:
A power of hell o'erclouds thy understanding.
I dare no longer stand in silence—dare
No longer see thee wandering on in darkness,
Nor pluck the bandage from thine eyes.
  Max.   My father!
Yet, ere thou speak'st, a moment's pause of
    thought!
If your disclosures should appear to be
Conjectures only—and almost I fear
They will be nothing further—spare them! I
Am not in that collected mood at present,
That I could listen to them quietly.
  Oct. The deeper cause thou hast to hate this
    light,
The more impatient cause have I, my son,
To force it on thee. To the innocence
And wisdom of thy heart I could have trusted
    thee
With calm assurance—but I see the net
Preparing—and it is thy heart itself
Alarms me for thine innocence—that secret,
    [*Fixing his eye steadfastly on his son's face.*
Which thou concealest, forces *mine* from me.
    [Max. *attempts to answer, but hesitates, and casts his eyes to the ground, embarrassed.*

Oct. [*after a pause.*] Know, then, they are
        duping thee!—a most foul game
With thee and with us all—nay, hear me calmly—
The Duke even now is playing. He assumes
The mask, as if he would forsake the army:
And in this moment makes he preparations
That army from the Emperor to *steal*,
And carry it over to the enemy!
  Max. That low priest's legend I know well, but
      did not
Expect to hear it from thy mouth.
  Oct.   That mouth,
From which thou hearest it at this present moment,
Doth warrant thee that it is no priest's legend.
  Max. How mere a maniac they supposed the
      Duke;
What, he can meditate?—the Duke?—can dream
That he can lure away full thirty thousand
Tried troops and true, all honourable soldiers,
More than a thousand noblemen among them,
From oaths, from duty, from their honour lure
      them,
And make them all unanimous to do
A deed that brands them scoundrels?
  Oct.   Such a deed
With such a front of infamy, the Duke
No wise desires—what he requires of us
Bears a far gentler appellation. Nothing
He wishes, but to give the Empire peace.

And so, because the Emperor hates *this* peace,
Therefore the Duke—the Duke will *force* him
  to it.
All parts of the Empire will he pacify,
And for his trouble will retain in payment
(What he has already in his gripe)—Bohemia!
 Max. Has he, Octavio, merited of us,
That we—that we should think so vilely of him?
 Oct. What *we would* think is not the question
  here.
The affair speaks for itself—and clearest proofs!
Hear me, my son—'tis not unknown to thee,
In what ill credit with the Court we stand.
But little dost thou know, or guess, what tricks,
What base intrigues, what lying artifices,
Have been employed—for this sole end—to sow
Mutiny in the camp! All bands are loosed—
Loosed all the bands, that link the officer
To his liege Emperor, all that bind the soldier
Affectionately to the citizen.
Lawless he stands, and threateningly beleaguers
The state he's bound to guard. To such a
  height
'Tis swoln, that at this hour the Emperor
Before his armies—his own armies—trembles;
Yea, in his capital, his palace, fears
The traitor's poniards, and is meditating
To hurry off and hide his tender offspring——
Not from the Swedes, not from the Lutherans—
No; from his own troops hide and hurry them!

Max. Cease, cease! thou torturest, shatter'st me. I know
That oft we tremble at an empty terror;
But the false phantasm brings a real misery.

Oct. It is no phantasm. An intestine war,
Of all the most unnatural and cruel,
Will burst out into flames, if instantly
We do not fly and stifle it. The Generals
Are many of them long ago won over;
The subalterns are vacillating—whole
Regiments and garrisons are vacillating.
To foreigners our strong-holds are entrusted;
To that suspected Schafgotch is the whole
Force of Silesia given up: to Tertsky
Five regiments, foot and horse—to Isolani,
To Illo, Kinsky, Butler, the best troops.

Max. Likewise to both of us.

Oct. Because the Duke
Believes he has secured us—means to lure us,
Still further on by splendid promises.
To me he portions forth the princedoms, Glatz
And Sagan; and too plain I see the angle
With which he doubts not to catch *thee.*

Max. No! no!
I tell thee—no!

Oct. O open yet thine eyes!
And to what purpose think'st thou he has called us
Hither to Pilsen?—to avail himself
Of our advice?—O when did Friedland ever

Need our advice?—Be calm, and listen to me.
To sell ourselves are we called hither, and,
Decline we that—to be his hostages.
Therefore doth noble Galas stand aloof!
Thy father, too, thou would'st not have seen here,
If higher duties had not held him fettered.

   Max. He makes no secret of it—needs make
        none—
That we're called hither for his sake—he owns it.
He needs our aidance to maintain himself—
He did so much for us; and 'tis but fair
That we too should do somewhat now for him.

   Oct. And know'st thou what it is which we
        must do?
That Illo's drunken mood betrayed it to thee.
Bethink thyself—what hast thou heard, what
    seen?
The counterfeited paper—the omission
Of that particular clause, so full of meaning,
Does it not prove, that they would bind us down
To nothing good?

   Max.   That counterfeited paper
Appears to me no other than a trick
Of Illo's own device. These underhand
Traders in great men's interests ever use
To urge and hurry all things to the extreme.
They see the Duke at variance with the court,
And fondly think to serve him, when they widen
The breach irreparably. Trust me, father,
The Duke knows nothing of all this.

Oct.   It grieves me
That I must dash to earth, that I must shatter
A faith so specious; but I may not spare thee!
For this is not a time for tenderness.
Thou must take measures, speedy ones—must act.
I therefore will confess to thee, that all
Which I've entrusted to thee now—that all
Which seems to thee so unbelievable,
That—yes, I will tell thee—[*A pause.*] Max.! I
    had it all.
From his own mouth—from the Duke's mouth I
    had it.
    Max. [*in excessive agitation.*] No!—no!—
    never!
    Oct.   Himself confided to me,
What I, 'tis true, had long before discovered
By other means—himself confided to me,
That 'twas his settled plan to join the Swedes;
And, at the head of the united armies,
Compel the Emperor——
    Max.   He is passionate,
The Court has stung him—he is sore all over
With injuries and affronts; and in a moment
Of irritation, what if he, for once,
Forgot himself? He's an impetuous man.
    Oct. Nay, in cold blood he did confess this to me:
And having construed my astonishment
Into a scruple of his power, he showed me
His written evidences—showed me letters,
Both from the Saxon and the Swede, that gave

Promise of aidance, and defin'd th' amount.

Max. It cannot be!—can *not* be! *can* not be!
Dost thou not see, it cannot!
Thou wouldest of necessity have shown him
Such horror, such deep loathing—that or he
Had tak'n thee for his better genius, or
Thou stood'st not now a living man before me—

Oct. I have laid open my objections to him,
Dissuaded him with pressing earnestness;
But my *abhorrence*, the full sentiment
Of my *whole* heart—that I have still kept sacred
To my own consciousness.

Max. And *thou* hast been
So treacherous! That looks not like my father!
I trusted not thy words, when thou didst tell me
Evil of him; much less can I *now* do it,
That thou calumniatest thy own self.

Oct. I did not thrust myself into his secrecy.

Max. Uprightness merited his confidence.

Oct. He was no longer worthy of sincerity.

Max. Dissimulation, sure, was still less worthy
Of thee, Octavio!

Oct. Gave I him a cause
To entertain a scruple of my honour?

Max. That he did not, evinc'd his confidence.

Oct. Dear son, it is not always possible
Still to preserve that infant purity
Which the voice teaches in our inmost heart.
Still in alarm, for ever on the watch
Against the wiles of wicked men, e'en Virtue

Will sometimes bear away her outward robes
Soiled in the wrestle with Iniquity.
This is the curse of every evil deed,
That, propagating still, it brings forth evil.
I do not cheat my better soul with sophisms:
I but perform my orders; the Emperor
Prescribes my conduct to me. Dearest boy,
Far better were it, doubtless, if we all
Obeyed the heart at all times; but so doing,
In this our present sojourn with bad men,
We must abandon many an honest object.
'Tis now our call to serve the Emperor,
By what means he can best be served—the heart
May whisper what it will—this is our call!

Max. It seems a thing appointed, that to-day
I should not comprehend, not understand thee.
The Duke thou say'st did honestly pour out
His heart to thee, but for an evil purpose;
And thou dishonestly hast cheated him
For a good purpose! Silence, I entreat thee—
My friend thou stealest not from me—
Let me not lose my father!

Oct. [*suppressing resentment.*] As yet thou
      know'st not all, my son. I have
Yet somewhat to disclose to thee. [*After a pause.*
                      Duke Friedland
Hath made his preparations. He relies
Upon his stars. He deems us unprovided,
And thinks to fall upon us by surprise.
Yea, in his dream of hope, he grasps already

The golden circle in his hand.   He errs.
We too have been in action—he but grasps
His evil fate, most evil, most mysterious!
    Max. O nothing rash, my sire!   By all that's good
Let me invoke thee—no precipitation!
    Oct. With light tread stole he on his evil way,
With light tread Vengeance stole on after him.
Unseen she stands already, dark behind him—
But one step more—he shudders in her grasp!
Thou hast seen Questenberg with me.   As yet
Thou know'st but his ostensible commission;
He brought with him a *private* one, my son!
And that was for me only.
    Max.   May I know it?
    Oct. [*seizes the patent.*]   Max!
                                       [*A pause*
——In this disclosure place I in thy hands
The Empire's welfare and thy father's life.
Dear to thy inmost heart is Wallenstein:
A powerful tie of love, of veneration,
Hath knit thee to him from thy earliest youth.
Thou nourishest the *wish.*—O let me still
Anticipate thy loitering confidence!
The *hope* thou nourishest to knit thyself
Yet closer to him——
    Max.   Father——
    Oct.   O my son,
I trust thy heart undoubtingly.   But am I
Equally sure of thy collectedness?

Wilt thou be able, with calm countenance,
To enter this man's presence, when that I
Have trusted to thee his whole fate?

Max. According
As thou dost trust me, father, with his crime.

[Octavio *takes a paper out of his escrutoire, and gives it to him.*

Max. What? how? a full Imperial patent!

Oct. Read it.

Max. [*just glances on it.*] Duke Friedland sentenced and condemned!

Oct. Even so.

Max. [*throws down the paper.*] O this is too much! O unhappy error!

Oct. Read on. Collect thyself.

Max. [*after he has read further, with a look of affright and astonishment on his father.*] How! what! Thou! thou!

Oct. But for the present moment, till the King
Of Hungary may safely join the army,
Is the command assigned to me.

Max. And think'st thou,
Dost thou believe, that thou wilt tear it from him?
O never hope it!—Father! father! father!
An inauspicious office is enjoined thee.
This paper here—this! and wilt thou enforce it?
The mighty in the middle of his host,
Surrounded by his thousands, him would'st thou
Disarm—degrade! Thou art lost, both thou and
all of us.

Oct. What hazard I incur thereby, I know.
In the great hand of God I stand. The Al-
    mighty
Will cover with his shield the Imperial house,
And shatter, in his wrath, the work of darkness.
The Emperor hath true servants still; and even
Here in the camp, there are enough brave men,
Who for the good cause will fight gallantly.
The faithful have been warned—the dangerous
Are closely watched. I wait but the first step,
And then immediately——

Max. What! on suspicion?
Immediately?

Oct. The Emperor is no tyrant.
The deed alone he'll punish, not the wish.
The Duke hath yet his destiny in his power.
Let him but leave the treason uncompleted,
He will be silently displaced from office,
And make way to his Emperor's royal son.
An honourable exile to his castles
Will be a benefaction to him rather
Than punishment. But the first open step—

Max. What callest thou such a step?
    wicked step
Ne'er will he take; but thou might'st easily,
Yea, thou hast done it, misinterpret him.

Oct. Nay, howsoever punishable were
Duke Friedland's purposes, yet still the steps
Which he·hath taken openly, permit
A mild construction. It is my intention

To leave this paper wholly uninforced
Till some act is committed which convicts him
Of a high treason, without doubt or plea,
And that shall sentence him.
 Max.   But who the judge?
 Oct. Thyself.
 Max. For ever, then, this paper will lie idle.
 Oct. Too soon, I fear, its powers must all be
  proved.
After the counter-promise of this evening,
It cannot be but he must deem himself
Secure of the majority with *us*;
And of the army's general sentiment
He hath a pleasing proof in that petition
Which thou deliveredst to him from the regiments.
Add this too—I have letters that the Rhinegrave
Hath changed his route, and travels by forced
  marches
To the Bohemian Forest. What this purports,
Remains unknown; and, to confirm suspicion,
This night a Swedish nobleman arrived here.
 Max. I have thy word. Thou'lt not proceed
  to action
Before thou hast convinced me—me myself.
 Oct. Is it possible? Still, after all thou know'st,
Canst thou believe still in his innocence?
 Max. [*with enthusiasm.*] Thy judgment may
  mistake; my heart can not.
    [*Moderates his voice and manner.*
These reasons might expound thy spirit or mine;

But they expound not Friedland—I have faith:
For as he knits his fortunes to the stars,
Even so doth he resemble them in secret,
Wonderful, still inexplicable courses!
Trust me, they do him wrong.   All will be solved.
These smokes, at once, will kindle into flame—
The edges of this black and stormy cloud
Will brighten suddenly, and we shall view
The Unapproachable glide out in splendour.

   Oct. I will await it.

SCENE II.—OCTAVIO *and* MAX. *as before.   To them the*
        Valet of the Chamber.

  Oct. How now, then?
  Val.   A dispatch is at the door.
  Oct. So early? From whom comes he then?
      Who is it?
  Val. That he refused to tell me.
  Oct.   Lead him in:
And hark you—let it not transpire.
        [*Exit* Valet—*the* Cornet *steps in.*
Ha! Cornet—is it you? and from Count Galas?
Give me your letters.
  Cor.   The Lieutenant-General
Trusted it not to letters.
  Oct.   And what is it?
  Cor. He bade me tell you—Dare I speak
      openly here?
  Oct. My son knows all.
  Cor.   We have him.

Oct. Whom?

Cor. Sesina,
The old negotiator.

Oct. [*eagerly.*] And you have him?

Cor. In the Bohemian Forest Captain Mohr-
brandt
Found and secured him yester morning early:
He was proceeding then to Regenspurg,
And on him were dispatches for the Swede.

Oct. And the dispatches——

Cor. The Lieutenant-General
Sent them that instant to Vienna, and
The prisoner with them.

Oct. This is, indeed, a tiding!
That fellow is a precious casket to us,
Inclosing weighty things—Was much found on
him?

Cor. I think, six packets, with Count Tertsky's
arms.

Oct. None in the Duke's own hand?

Cor. Not that I know.

Oct. And old Sesina?

Cor. He was sorely frightened,
When it was told him he must to Vienna.
But the Count Altringer bade him take heart,
Would he but make a full and free confession.

Oct. Is Altringer then with your Lord? I
heard
That he lay sick at Linz.

Cor. These three days past

He's with my master, the Lieutenant-General,
At Frauemburg. Already have they sixty
Small companies together, chosen men ;
Respectfully they greet you with assurances,
That they are only waiting your commands.

   Oct. In a few days may great events take place.
And when must you return?
   Cor.   I wait your orders.
   Oct. Remain till evening.

    [CORNET *signifies his assent and obesiance, and is going.*

                       No one saw you—ha?
   Cor. No living creature. Through the cloister
       wicket
The Capuchins, as usual, let me in.
   Oct. Go, rest your limbs, and keep yourself
       concealed.
I hold it probable, that yet ere evening
I shall dispatch you. The development
Of this affair approaches: ere the day,
That even now is dawning in the heaven,
Ere this eventful day hath set, the lot
That must decide our fortunes will be drawn.

                            [*Exit* Cornet.

SCENE III.—OCTAVIO, *and* MAX. PICCOLOMINI.

   Oct. Well—and what now, son? All will soon
       be clear ;
For all, I'm certain, went through that Sesina.

Max. [*who through the whole of the foregoing scene has been in a visible struggle of feelings, at length starts as one resolved.*] I will procure me light a shorter way.   Farewell.

  Oct.   Where now?—Remain here.
  Max. To the Duke.
  Oct. [*alarmed.*]   What——
  Max. [*returning.*] If thou hast believed that I
    shall act
A part in this thy play——
Thou hast miscalculated on me grievously.
My way must be straight on.   True with the
  tongue,
False with the heart—I may not, cannot be:
Nor can I suffer that a man should trust me—
As his friend trust me—and then lull my con-
  science
With such low pleas as these:—" I ask'd him
  not—
He did it all at his own hazard—and
My *mouth* has never lied to him."—No, no!
What a friend takes me for, that I must be:
—I'll to the Duke; ere yet this day is ended
Will I demand of him that he do save
His good name from the world, and with one
  stride
Break through and rend this fine-spun web of
  yours.
He can, he will;—*I* still am his believer.
Yet I'll not pledge myself, but that those letters

May furnish you, perchance, with proofs against
    him.
How far may not this Tertsky have proceeded—
What may not he himself too have permitted
Himself to do, to snare the enemy,
The laws of war excusing? Nothing, save
His own mouth shall convict him—nothing less!
And face to face will I go question him.

  Oct. Thou wilt?

  Max.   I will, as sure as this heart beats.

  Oct. I have, indeed, miscalculated on thee.
I calculated on a prudent son,
Who would have bless'd the hand beneficent
That plucked him back from the abyss—and lo!
A fascinated being I discover,
Whom his two eyes befool, whom passion wilders,
Whom not the broadest light of noon can heal.
Go, question him!—Be mad enough, I pray thee.
The purpose of thy father, of thy Emperor,
Go, give it up free booty:—Force me, drive me
To an open breach before the time. And now,
Now that a miracle of heaven had guarded
My secret purpose even to this hour,
And laid to sleep suspicion's piercing eyes,
Let me have lived to see that mine own son,
With frantic enterprise, annihilates
My toilsome labours and state policy.

  Max. Ay—this state policy! O how I curse it!
You will some time, with your state policy,
Compel him to the measure: it may happen,

Because ye are *determined* that he is guilty,
Guilty ye'll *make* him. All retreat cut off,
You close up every outlet, hem him in
Narrower and narrower, till at length ye force
    him—
Yes, *ye*—ye *force* him, in his desperation,
To set fire to his prison.   Father! Father!
That never can end well—it cannot—will not!
And let it be decided as it may,
I see with boding heart the near approach
Of an ill-starred, unblest catastrophe.
For this great monarch-spirit, if he fall,
Will drag a world into the ruin with him.
And as a ship (that midway on the ocean
Takes fire) at once, and with a thunder-burst
Explodes, and with itself shoots out its crew
In smoke and ruin betwixt sea and heaven;
So will he, falling, draw down in his fall
All us, who're fixed and mortised to his fortune.
Deem of it what thou wilt; but pardon me,
That I must bear me on in my own way.
All must remain pure betwixt him and me;
And, ere the day-light dawns, it must be known
Which I must lose—my father, or my friend.

[*During his exit the curtain drops.*

ACT IV.

Scene I.— *A Room fitted up for astrological labours, and provided with celestial charts, with globes, telescopes, quadrants, and other mathematical instruments.—Seven colossal figures, representing the planets, each with a transparent star of a different colour on its head, stand in a semicircle in the background, so that Mars and Saturn are nearest the eye.—The remainder of the Scene, and its disposition, is given in the Fourth Scene of the Second Act.—There must be a curtain over the figures, which may be dropped, and conceal them on occasions.*
[*In the Fifth Scene of this Act it must be dropped; but in the Seventh Scene, it must be again drawn up wholly or in part.*]
Wallenstein *at a black table, on which a Speculum Astrologicum is described with chalk.* Seni *is taking observations through a window.*

Wal. All well—and now let it be ended, Seni.—
    Come,
The dawn commences, and Mars rules the hour.
We must give o'er the operation. Come,
We know enough.
  Seni. Your Highness must permit me
Just to contemplate Venus. She's now rising:
Like as a sun, so shines she in the east.
  Wal. She is at present in her perigee,
And shoots down now her strongest influences.
        [*Contemplating the figure on the table.*

Auspicious aspect! fateful in conjunction,
At length the mighty three corradiate;
And the two stars of blessing, Jupiter
And Venus, take between them the malignant
Slily-malicious Mars, and thus compel
Into *my* service that old mischief-founder;
For long he viewed me hostilely, and ever
With beam oblique, or perpendicular,
Now in the Quartile, now in the Secundan,
Shot his red lightnings at my stars, disturbing
Their blessèd influences and sweet aspects.
Now they have conquered the old enemy,
And bring him in the heavens a prisoner to me.

   Seni. [*who has come down from the window.*]
And in a corner house, your Highness—think of
      that!
That makes each influence of double strength.

   Wal. And sun and moon, too, in the Sextile
      aspect,
The soft light with the veh'ment—so I love it.
Sol is the heart, Luna the head of heaven,
Bold be the plan, fiery the execution.

   Seni. And both the mighty Lumina by no
Maleficus affronted. Lo! Saturnus,
Innocuous, powerless, in cadente Domo.

   Wal. The empire of Saturnus is gone by:
Lord of the secret birth of things is he;
Within the lap of earth, and in the depths
Of the imagination dominates;
And his are all things that eschew the light.

The time is o'er of brooding and contrivance;
For Jupiter, the lustrous, lordeth now,
And the dark work, complete of preparation,
He draws by force into the realm of light.
Now must we hasten on to action, ere
The scheme, and most auspicious positure
Parts o'er my head, and takes once more its flight;
For the heavens journey still, and sojourn not.

              [*There are knocks at the door.*

There's some one knocking there. See who it is.
  Tertsky. [*from without.*] Open, and let me in.
  Wal.   Ay—'tis Tertsky.
What is there of such urgency? We are busy.
  Ter. [*from without.*] Lay all aside at present,
      I entreat you.
It suffers no delaying.
  Wal.   Open, Seni!

    [*While* SENI *opens the door for* TERTSKY, WALLEN-
      STEIN *draws the curtain over the figures.*

  Ter. [*enters.*] Hast thou already heard it? He
      is taken.
Galas has given him up to the Emperor.
           [SENI *draws off the black table and exit.*

      SCENE II.—WALLENSTEIN, COUNT TERTSKY.

  Wal. [*to Tertsky.*] Who has been taken?—Who
      is given up?
  Ter. The man who knows our secrets, who
      knows every

Negotiation with the Swede and Saxon,
Through whose hands all and every thing has
   passed—
 Wal. [*drawing back.*] Nay, not Sesina?—Say,
  No! I entreat thee.
 Ter. All on his road for Regenspurg to the
  Swede
He was plunged down upon by Galas' agent,
Who had been long in ambush, lurking for him.
There must have been found on him my whole
   packet
To Thur, to Kinsky, to Oxenstirn, to Arnheim:
All this is in their hands; they have now an
   insight
Into the whole—our measures, and our motives.

  SCENE III.—*To them enters* ILLO.

 Illo. [*to* TERTSKY.] Has he heard it?
 Ter. He has heard it.
 Illo [*to* WALLENSTEIN.] Thinkest thou still
To make thy peace with the Emp'ror, to regain
His confidence?—E'en were it now thy wish
To abandon all thy plans, yet still they know
What thou hast wished; then forwards thou must
   press!
Retreat is now no longer in thy power.
 Ter. They have documents against us, and in
  hands,
Which show beyond all power of contradiction—

Wal. Of my handwriting—no iota.   Thee
I punish for thy lies.
   Illo.   And thou believest,
That what this man, that what thy sister's husband,
Did in thy name, will not stand on thy reck'ning?
His word must pass for thy word with the Swede,
And not with those that hate thee at Vienna.
   Ter. In writing thou gav'st nothing—But be-
        think thee,
How far thou venturedst by word of mouth
With this Sesina?   And will he be silent?
If he can save himself by yielding up
Thy secret purposes, will he retain them?
   Illo. Thyself dost not conceive it possible;
And since they now have evidence authentic
How far thou hast already gone, speak!—tell us,
What art thou waiting for? thou canst no longer
Keep thy command; and beyond hope of rescue
Thou'rt lost, if thou resign'st it.
   Wal.   In the army
Lies my security.   The army will not
Abandon me. Whatever they may know,
The power is mine, and they must gulp it down—
And substitute I caution for my fealty,
They must be satisfied, at least appear so.
   Illo. The army, Duke, *is* thine now—for this
        moment—
'Tis thine: but think with terror on the slow,
The quiet power of time.   From open violence
The attachment of thy soldiery secures thee

To-day—to-morrow; but grant'st thou them a
  respite,
Unheard, unseen, they'll undermine that love
On which thou now dost feel so firm a footing,
With wily theft will draw away from thee
One after th' other——

 Wal.   'Tis a cursed accident!

 Illo. O, I will call it a most blessed one,
If it work on thee as it ought to do,
Hurry thee on to action—to decision.
The Swedish General——

 Wal.   He's arrived! Know'st thou
What his commission is——

 Illo.   To thee alone
Will he entrust the purpose of his coming.

 Wal. A cursed, cursed accident! Yes, yes,
Sesina knows too much, and won't be silent.

 Ter. He's a Bohemian fugitive and rebel,
His neck is forfeit. Can he save himself
At thy cost, think you he will scruple it?
And if they put him to the torture, will he,
Will *he*, that dastardling, have strength
  enough——

 Wal. [*lost in thought.*] Their confidence is lost—
  irreparably!
And I may act what way I will, I shall
Be and remain for ever in their thought
A traitor to my country. How sincerely
Soever I return back to my duty,
It will no longer help me——

Illo.   Ruin thee,
That it will do! Not thy fidelity,
Thy weakness will be deemed the sole occasion—
   Wal. [*pacing up and down in extreme agita-
   tion.*] What! I must realize it now in earnest,
Because I toyed too freely with the thought?
Accursed he who dallies with a devil!
And must I—I *must* realize it now—
Now, while I have the power, it *must* take place?
   Illo. Now—now—ere they can ward and par-
   ry it!
   Wal. [*looking at the paper of signatures.*] I
   have the Generals' word—a written promise!
Max. Piccolomini stands not here—how's that?
   Ter. It was——he fancied——
   Illo.   Mere self-willedness.
There needed no such thing 'twixt him and you.
   Wal. He is quite right—there needeth no such
   thing,
The regiments, too, deny to march for Flanders—
Have sent me in a paper of remonstrance,
And openly resist the Imperial orders.
The first step to revolt's already taken.
   Illo. Believe me, thou wilt find it far more easy
To lead them over to the enemy
Than to the Spaniard.
   Wal.   I will hear, however,
What the Swede has to say to me.
   Illo. [*eagerly to* TERTSKY.]   Go, call him!
He stands without the door in waiting.

Wal.   Stay!
Stay yet a little. It hath taken me
All by surprise,—it came too quick upon me;
'Tis wholly novel, that an accident,
With its dark lordship, and blind agency,
Should force me on with it.

  Illo.   First hear him only,
And after weigh it.   [*Exeunt* TERTSKY *and* ILLO.

SCENE IV.—WALLENSTEIN.

Wal. [*in soliloquy.*] Is it possible?
Is't so? I *can* no longer what I *would!*
No longer draw back at my liking! I
Must *do* the deed, because I *thought* of it,
And fed this heart here with a dream! Because
I did not scowl temptation from my presence,
Dallied with thoughts of possible fulfilment,
Commenced no movement, left all time uncertain,
And only kept the road, the access open!
By the great God of Heaven! it was not
My serious meaning, it was ne'er resolve.
I but amused myself with thinking of it.
The free-will tempted me, the power to do
Or not to do it.—Was it criminal
To make the fancy minister to hope,
To fill the air with pretty toys of air,
And clutch fantastic sceptres moving t'ward me?
Was not the will kept free? Beheld I not
The road of duty close beside me—but

One little step, and once more I was in it!
Where am I? Whither have I been transported?
No road, no track behind me, but a wall,
Impenetrable, insurmountable,
Rises obedient to the spells I muttered
And meant not—my own doings tower behind me.
            [*Pauses, and remains in deep thought.*

A punishable man I seem, the guilt,
Try what I will, I cannot roll off from me;
The equivocal demeanour of my life
Bears witness on my prosecutor's party;
And even my purest acts from purest motives
Suspicion poisons with malicious gloss.
Were I that thing, for which I pass, that traitor,
A goodly outside I had sure reserved,
Had drawn the cov'rings thick and double round
    me,
Been calm and chary of my utterance.
But being conscious of the innocence
Of my intent, my uncorrupted will,
I gave way to my humours, to my passion:
Bold were my words, because my deeds were *not*.
Now every planless measure, chance event,
The threat of rage, the vaunt of joy and triumph,
And all the May-games of a heart o'erflowing,
Will they connect, and weave them all together
Into one web of treason; all will be plan,
My eye ne'er absent from the far-off mark,
Step tracing step, each step a politic progress;
And out of all they'll fabricate a charge

So specious, that I must myself stand *dumb*.
I am caught in my own net, and only force,
Nought but a sudden *rent* can liberate me.

        [*Pauses again.*

How else! since that the heart's unbiased instinct
Impelled me to the daring deed, which now
Necessity, self-preservation, *orders*.
Stern is the on-look of Necessity,
Not without shudder many a human hand
Grasps the mysterious urn of destiny.
My deed was mine, remaining in my bosom,
Once suffered to escape from its safe corner
Within the heart, its nursery and birthplace,
Sent forth into the foreign, it belongs
For ever to those sly malicious powers
Whom never art of man conciliated.

  [*Paces in agitation through the Chamber, then pauses,
   and, after the pause, breaks out again into audible
   soliloquy.*

What is thy enterprise? thy aim? thy object?
Hast honestly confessed it to thyself?
Power seated on a quiet throne thou'dst shake,
Power of an ancient consecrated throne,
Strong in possession, founded in old custom;
Power by a thousand tough and stringy roots
Fixed to the people's pious nursery-faith.
This, this will be no strife of strength with strength.
That feared I not. I brave each combatant,
Whom I can look on, fixing eye to eye,
Who, full himself of courage, kindles courage

In me too. 'Tis a foe invisible,
The which I fear—a fearful enemy,
Which in the human heart opposes me,
By its coward fear alone made fearful to me.
Not that, which full of life, instinct with power,
Makes known its present being, that is not
The true, the perilously formidable.
O no! it is the common, the quite common,
The thing of an eternal yesterday,
What ever was, and evermore returns,
Sterling to-morrow, for to-day 'twas sterling!
For of the wholly common is man made,
And custom is his nurse! Woe then to them,
Who lay irreverent hands upon his old
House furniture, the dear inheritance
From his forefathers. For time consecrates;
And what is gray with age becomes religion.
Be in possession, and thou hast the right,
And sacred will the many guard it for thee!

[*To the* Page *who here enters.*

The Swedish officer?—Well, let him enter.

[*The* Page *exit,* WALLENSTEIN *fixes his eye in deep thought on the door.*

Yet is it pure—as yet!—the crime has come
Not o'er this threshold yet—so slender is
The boundary that divideth life's two paths.

SCENE V.—WALLENSTEIN *and* WRANGEL.

Wal. [*after having fixed a searching look on him.*] Your name is Wrangel?

Wran. Gustave Wrangel, General
Of the Sudermanian Blues.

Wal. It was a Wrangel
Who injured me materially at Stralsund,
And by his brave resistance was the cause
Of th' opposition which that seaport made.

Wran. It was the doing of the element
With which you fought, my lord! and not my merit.
The Baltic Neptune did assert his freedom,
The sea and land, it seemed, were not to serve
One and the same.

Wal. [*makes a motion for him to take a seat, and seats himself.*] And where are your credentials?
Come you provided with full powers, Sir General?

Wran. There are so many scruples yet to solve——

Wal. [*having read the credentials.*] An able letter!—Ay—he is a prudent,
Intelligent master, whom you serve, Sir General!
The Chancellor writes me, that he but fulfils
His late departed Sovereign's own idea
In helping me to the Bohemian crown.

Wran. He says the truth. Our great king, now in heaven,
Did ever deem most highly of your Grace's
Preëminent sense and military genius;
And always the commanding Intellect,
He said, should have command, and be the king.

Wal. Yes, he *might* say it safely.—General
       Wrangel,   [*Taking his hand affectionately.*
Come, fair and open—Trust me, I was always
A Swede at heart. Ey! that did you experience
Both in Silesia and at Nuremburg;
I had you often in my power, and let you
Always slip out by some back door or other.
'Tis this for which the Court can ne'er forgive me,
Which drives me to this present step: and since
Our interests so run in one direction,
E'en let us have a thorough confidence
Each in the other.
    Wran.   Confidence will come,
Has each but only first security.
    Wal. The Chancellor still, I see, does not quite
        trust me;
And, I confess—the gain does not lie wholly
To my advantage—Without doubt he thinks
If I can play false with the Emperor,
Who is my sovereign, I can do the like
With th' enemy, and that *the one* too were
Sooner to be forgiven me than the *other*.
Is not this your opinion too, Sir General?
    Wran. I have here an office merely, no opinion.
    Wal. The Emperor hath urged me to the
        uttermost.
I can no longer honourably serve him.
For my security, in self-defence,
I take this hard step, which my conscience blames.
    Wran. That I believe. So far would no one go

Who was not forced to it.   [*After a pause.*
                    What may have impelled
Your princely Highness in this wise to act
Toward your Sovereign Lord and Emperor,
Beseems not us to expound or criticize.
The Swede is fighting for his good old cause,
With his good sword and conscience. This concurrence,
This opportunity, is in our favour,
And all advantages in war are lawful.
We take what offers without questioning;
And if all have its due and just proportions——
   Wal. Of what then are ye doubting? Of my will?
Or of my power? I pledge me to the Chancellor,
Would he trust *me* with sixteen thousand men,
That I would instantly go over to them
With eighteen thousand of the Emperor's troops.
   Wran. Your Grace is known to be a mighty war-chief,
To be a second Attila and Pyrrhus.
'Tis talked of still with fresh astonishment,
How some years past, beyond all human faith
You called an army forth, like a creation;
But yet——
   Wal.   But yet?
   Wran.   But still the Chancellor thinks,
It might yet be an easier thing from nothing
To call forth sixty thousand men of battle,
Than to persuade one sixtieth part of them—

Wal. What now? Out with it, friend?
Wran.   To break their oaths.
Wal. And he thinks *so?*—He judges like a
    Swede,
And like a Protestant. You Lutherans
Fight for your Bible. You are int'rested
About the cause; and with your *hearts* you follow
Your banners.—Among *you,* whoe'er deserts
To the enemy, hath broken covenant
With two Lords at one time. We've no such fancies.
    Wran. Great God in Heaven! Have then the
        people here
No house and home, no fireside, no altar?
    Wal. I will explain that to you, how it stands—
The Austrian *has* a country, ay, and loves it,
And has good cause to love it—but this army,
That calls itself th' Imperial, this that houses
Here in Bohemia, this has none—no country;
This is an outcast of all foreign lands,
Unclaimed by town or tribe, to whom belongs
Nothing, except the universal sun.
    Wran. But then the nobles and the officers?
Such a desertion, such a felony,
It is without example, my Lord Duke,
In the world's history.
    Wal.   They are all mine—
Mine unconditionally, mine on all terms.
Not me, your own eyes you must trust.

  [*He gives him the paper containing the written oath.*
    WRANGEL *reads it through, and having read it,
    lays it on the table, remaining silent.*

				So then?
Now comprehend you?
  Wran.			Comprehend who can!
My Lord Duke; I will let the mask drop—yes!
I've full powers for a final settlement.
The Rhinegrave stands but four days' march
			from here
With fifteen thousand men, and only waits
For orders to proceed and join your army.
Those orders *I* give out, immediately
We're compromised.
  Wal.			What asks the Chancellor?
  Wran. [*considerately.*] Twelve regiments,
			every man a Swede—my head
The warranty—and all might prove at last
Only false play——
  Wal. [*starting.*] Sir Swede!
  Wran. [*calmly proceeding.*] Am therefore
			forced
T' insist thereon, that he do formally,
Irrevocably break with th' Emperor,
Else not a Swede is trusted to Duke Friedland.
  Wal. Come, brief and open! what is the
			demand?
  Wran. That he forthwith disarm the Spanish
			reg'ments
Attached to th' Emperor, that he seize Prague,
And to the Swedes give up that city, with
The strong pass Egra.
  Wal.			That is much indeed!

Prague!—Egra's granted—But—but Prague!—
    'Twon't do.
I give you every security
Which you may ask of me in common reason—
But Prague—Bohemia—these, Sir General,
I can myself protect.
    Wran.   We doubt it not.
But 'tis not the protection that is now
Our sole concern. We want security,
That we shall not expend our men and money
All to no purpose.
    Wal.   'Tis but reasonable.
    Wran. And till we are indemnified, so long
Stays Prague in pledge.
    Wal.   Then trust you us so little?
    Wran. [*rising.*] The Swede, if he would treat
    well with the German,
Must keep a sharp look out. We have been
    called
Over the Baltic, we have saved the empire
From ruin—with our best blood have we sealed
The liberty of faith, and gospel truth.
But now already is the benefaction
No longer felt, the load alone is felt.——
Ye look askance with evil eye upon us,
As foreigners, intruders in the empire,
And would fain send us, with some paltry
Of money, home again to our old forests.
No no! my Lord Duke! no!—it never was
For Judas' pay, for chinking gold and silver,

That we did leave our king by the great Stone.*
No, not for gold and silver have there bled
So many of our Swedish nobles—neither
Will we, with empty laurels for our payment,
Hoist sail for our own country. *Citizens*
Will we remain upon the soil, the which
Our monarch conquered for himself, and died.

   Wal. Help to keep down the common enemy,
And the fair border land must needs be yours.

   Wran. But when the common enemy lies
      vanquished,
Who knits together our new friendship then?
We know, Duke Friedland! though perhaps the
      Swede
Ought not t'have known it, that you carry on
Secret negotiations with the Saxons.
Who is our warranty, that *we* are not
The sacrifices in those articles
Which 'tis thought needful to conceal from us?

   Wal. [*rises.*] Think you of something better,
      Gustave Wrangel!
Of Prague no more.

   Wran.   Here my commission ends.

   Wal. Surrender up to you my capital!
Far liever would I face about, and step
Back to my Emperor.

   Wran.   If time yet permits——

---

* A great stone near Lutzen, since called the Swede's Stone, the body of their great king having been found at the foot of it, after the battle in which he lost his life.

Wal. That lies with me, even now, at any hour.
Wran. Some days ago, perhaps. To day, no
   longer,
No longer since Sesina is a prisoner.
   [WALLENSTEIN *is struck, and silenced.*
My Lord Duke hear me—We believe that you
At present do mean honourably by us.
Since *yesterday* we're sure of that—and now
This paper warrants for the troops, there's
   nothing
Stands in the way of our full confidence.
Prague shall not part us. Hear! The Chan-
   cellor
Contents himself with Albstadt, to your Grace
He gives up Ratschin and the narrow side.
But Egra above all must open to us,
Ere we can think of any junction.
   Wal.   You,
You, therefore must I trust, and you not me?
I will consider of your proposition.
   Wran. I must entreat, that your consideration
Occupy not too long a time. Already
Has this negotiation, my Lord Duke,
Crept on into the second year. If nothing
Is settled this time, will the Chancellor
Consider it as broken off for ever.
   Wal. Ye press me hard. A measure such as
      this,
Ought to be *thought* of.
   Wran.   Ay! but think of this too,

That sudden action only can procure it
Success—think first of this, your Highness.
        [*Exit* WRANGEL.

SCENE VI.—WALLENSTEIN TERTSKY, *and* ILLO (*re-enter.*)

 Illo. Is't all right?
 Ter.   Are you compromised?
 Illo.   This Swede
Went smiling from you. Yes! you're compromised.
 Wal. As yet is nothing settled: and (well weighed)
I feel myself inclined to leave it so.
 Ter. How? What is that?
 Wal.   Come on me what will come,
The doing evil to avoid an evil
Cannot be good!
 Ter.   Nay, but bethink you, Duke?
 Wal. To live upon the mercy of these Swedes!
Of these proud-hearted Swedes, I could not bear it.
 Illo. Goest thou as fugitive, as mendicant?
Bringest thou not more to them than thou receivest?

SCENE VII.—*To these Enter the* COUNTESS TERTSKY.

 Wal. Who sent for you? There is no business here
For women.
 Coun. I am come to bid you joy.

Wal. Use thy authority, Tertsky, bid her go.
Coun. Come I perhaps too early? I hope
 not.
Wal. Set not this tongue upon me, I entreat
 you.
You know it is the weapon that destroys me.
I am routed, if a woman but attack me.
I cannot traffic in the trade of words
With that unreasoning sex.
 Coun.   I had already
Given the Bohemians a king.
 Wal. [*sarcastically.*]   They have one,
In consequence, no doubt.
 Coun. [*to the others.*] Ha! what new scruple?
Ter. The Duke will not.
Coun.   He *will not* what he *must!*
Illo. It lies with you now. Try. For I am
 silenced,
When folks begin to talk to me of conscience
And of fidelity.
 Coun.   How? then, when all
Lay in the far off distance, when the road
Stretched out before thine eyes interminably,
Then hadst thou courage and resolve; and now,
Now that the dream is being realized,
The purpose ripe, the issue ascertained,
Dost thou begin to play the dastard now?
Planned merely, 'tis a common felony;
Accomplished, an immortal undertaking:
And with success comes pardon hand in hand;

For all event is God's arbitrament.
   Servant [*enters.*] The Colonel Piccolomini.
   Coun. [*hastily.*]   —Must wait.
   Wal. I cannot see him now. Another time.
   Ser. But for two minutes he entreats an
      audience.
Of the most urgent nature is his business.
   Wal. Who knows what he may bring us? I
      will hear him.
   Coun. (*laughs.*) Urgent for him, no doubt;
      but thou mayest wait.
   Wal. What is it?
   Coun.   Thou shalt be informed hereafter.
First let the Swede and thee be compromised.

                        [*Exit* Servant.

   Wal. If there were yet a choice! if yet some
      milder
Way of escape were possible—I still
Will choose it, and avoid the last extreme.
   Coun. Desir'st thou nothing further? Such a
      way
Lies still before thee. Send this Wrangel off.
Forget thou thy old hopes, cast far away
All thy past life; determine to commence
A new one. Virtue hath her heroes too,
As well as fame and fortune. To Vienna—
Hence—to the Emperor—kneel before the throne;
Take a full coffer with thee—say aloud,
Thou didst but wish to prove thy fealty;
Thy whole intention but to dupe the Swede.

Illo. For that too 'tis too late. They know too
    much.
He would but bear his own head to the block.
  Coun. I fear not that. They have not evidence
To attaint him legally, and they avoid
The avowal of an arbitrary power.
They'll let the Duke resign without disturbance.
I see how all will end. The King of Hungary
Makes his appearance, and 'twill of itself
Be understood, that then the Duke retires.
There will not want a formal declaration.
The young king will administer the oath
To the whole army; and so all returns
To the old position. On some morrow morning
The Duke departs; and now 'tis stir and bustle
Within his castles. He will hunt, and build,
Superintend his horses' pedigrees;
Creates himself a court, gives golden keys,
And introduceth strictest ceremony
In fine proportions, and nice etiquette;
Keeps open table with high cheer; in brief,
Commenceth mighty king—in miniature.
And while he prudently demeans himself,
And gives himself no actual importance,
He will be let appear whate'er he likes;
And who dares doubt, that Friedland will appear
A mighty prince to his last dying hour?
Well now, what then? Duke Friedland is as
    others
A fire-new noble, whom the war hath raised

To price and currency, a Jonah's gourd,
An over-night creation of court-favour,
Which with an undistinguishable ease
Makes baron or makes prince.
 Wal. [*in extreme agitation.*] Take her away.
Let in the young Count Piccolomini.
 Coun. Art thou in earnest? I entreat thee!
  Canst thou
Consent to bear thyself to thy own grave,
So ignominiously to be dried up?
Thy life, that arrogated such a height
To end in such a nothing! To be nothing,
When one was always nothing, is an evil
That asks no stretch of patience, a light evil,
But to become a nothing, having been——
 Wal. [*starts up in violent agitation.*] Show me
  a way out of this stifling crowd,
Ye powers of aidance! Show me such a way
As *I* am capable of going.—I
Am no tongue-hero, no fine virtue-prattler;
I cannot warm by thinking; cannot say
To the good luck that turns her back upon me,
Magnanimously: "Go; I need thee not."
Cease I to work, I am annihilated.
Dangers nor sacrifices will I shun,
If so I may avoid the last extreme;
But ere I sink down into nothingness,
Leave off so little, who began so great,
Ere that the world confuses me with those
Poor wretches, whom a day creates and crumbles,

This age and after-ages speak my name
With hate and dread; and Friedland be redemp-
      tion
For each accursed deed!
  Coun.   What is there here, then,
So against nature? Help me to perceive it!
O let not superstition's nightly goblins
Subdue thy clear bright spirit! Art thou bid
To murder?—with abhorred accursed poignard,
To violate the breasts that nourished thee?
That *were* against our nature, that might aptly
Make thy flesh shudder, and thy whole heart
      sicken;—
Yet not a few, and for a meaner object,
Have ventured even this, ay, and performed it.
What is there in thy case so black and monstrous?
Thou art accused of treason—whether with
Or without justice is not now the question—
Thou art lost if thou dost not avail thee quickly
Of the power which thou possessest—Friedland!
  Duke!
Tell me, where lives that thing so meek and tame,
That doth not all his living faculties
Put forth in preservation of his life?
What deed so daring, which necessity
And desperation will not sanctify?
  Wal. Once was this Ferdinand so gracious
      to me:
He loved me; he esteemed me; I was placed
The nearest to his heart. Full many a time

We like familiar friends, both at one table,
Have banqueted together.   He and I—
And the young kings themselves held me the basin
Wherewith to wash me—and is't come to this?
   Coun. So faithfully preserv'st thou each small favour,
And hast no memory for contumelies?
Must I remind thee, how at Regenspurg
This man repaid thy faithful services?
All ranks and all conditions in the empire
Thou hadst wronged, to make him great,—hadst loaded on thee,
On *thee*, the hate, the curse of the whole world.
No friend existed for thee in all Germany;
And why? because thou hadst existed only
For the Emperor.   To the Emperor alone
Clung Friedland in that storm which gathered round him
At Regenspurg in the Diet—and he dropped thee;
He let thee fall!   He let thee fall a victim
To the Bavarian, to that insolent!
Deposed, stript bare of all thy dignity
And power, amid the taunting of thy foes.
Thou wert let drop into obscurity.—
Say not, the restoration of thy honour
Hath made atonement for that first injustice.
No honest good-will was it that replaced thee,
The law of hard necessity replaced thee,

Which they had fain opposed, but that they could
   not.
 Wal. Not to their good wishes, that is certain,
Nor yet to his affection I'm indebted
For this high office ; and if I abuse it,
I shall therein abuse no confidence.
 Coun. Affection! confidence!—They *needed*
   thee.
Necessity, impetuous remonstrant!
Who not with empty names, or shows of proxy,
Is served, who'll have the thing and not the
   symbol,
Ever seeks out the greatest and the best,
And at the rudder places *him,* e'en though
She had been forced to take him from the rab-
   ble—
She, this necessity, it was that placed thee
In this high office, it was she that gave thee
Thy letters patent of inauguration.
For, to the uttermost moment that they can,
This race still help themselves at cheapest rate
With slavish souls, with puppets! At the approach
Of extreme peril, when a hollow image
Is found a hollow image and no more,
Then falls the power into the mighty hands
Of nature, of the spirit giant-born,
Who listens only to himself, knows nothing
Of stipulations, duties, reverences,
And, like the emancipated force of fire,
Unmastered scorches, ere it reaches them,

Their fine-spun webs, their artificial policy.

Wal. 'Tis true! they saw me always as I am—
Always! I did not cheat them in the bargain.
I never held it worth my pains to hide
The bold all-grasping habit of my soul.

Coun. Nay rather—thou hast ever shown
      thyself
A formidable man, without restraint;
Hast exercised the full prerogatives
Of thy impetuous nature, which had been
Once granted to thee. Therefore, Duke, not
      thou,
Who hast still remained consistent with thyself,
But *they* are in the wrong who fearing thee,
Entrusted such a power in hands they feared.
For, by the laws of spirit, in the right
Is every individual character
That acts in strict consistence with itself.
Self-contradiction is the only wrong.
Wert thou another being, then, when thou
Eight years ago pursuedst thy march with fire
And sword, and desolation, through the Circles
Of Germany, the universal scourge,
Didst mock all ordinances of the empire,
The fearful rights of strength alone exertedst,
Trampledst to earth each rank, each magistracy,
All to extend thy Sultan's domination?
Then was the time to break thee in, to curb
Thy haughty will, to teach thee ordinance.
But no! the Emperor felt no touch of conscience;

What served him pleased him, and without a
 murmur
He stamped his broad seal on these lawless deeds.
What at that time was right, because thou didst it
For him, to-day is all at once become
Opprobrious, foul, because it is directed
Against him.—O most flimsy superstition!
 Wal. [*rising.*] I never saw it in this light
  before.
'Tis even so. The Emperor perpetrated
Deeds through my arm, deeds most unorderly.
And even this prince's mantle, which I wear,
I owe to what were services to him,
But most high misdemeanours 'gainst the empire.
 Coun. Then betwixt thee and him (confess it,
  Friedland!)
The point can be no more of right and duty,
Only of power and opportunity.
That opportunity, lo! it comes yonder,
Approaching with swift steeds; then with a swing
Throw thyself up into the chariot seat,
Seize with firm hand the reins, ere thy opponent
Anticipate thee, and himself make conquest
Of the now empty seat. The moment comes—
It is already here, when thou must write
The absolute total of thy life's vast sum.
The constellations stand victorious o'er thee.
The planets shoot good fortune in fair junctions,
And tell thee, "Now's the time!" The starry
 courses

Hast thou thy life-long measured to no purpose?
The quadrant and the circle, were they playthings?
[*Pointing to the different objects in the room.*
The zodiacs, the rolling orbs, of heaven,
Hast pictured on these walls, and all around thee
In dumb, foreboding symbols hast thou placed
These seven presiding Lords of Destiny—
For toys? Is all this preparation nothing?
Is there no marrow in this hollow art,
That even to thyself it doth avail
Nothing, and has no influence over thee
In the great moment of decision?——

Wal. [*during this last speech walks up and down with inward struggles, labouring with passions; stops suddenly, stands still, then interrupting the Countess.*] Send Wrangel to me—I will instantly
Dispatch three couriers——

Illo. [*hurrying out.*] God in heaven be praised!

Wal. It is his evil genius and mine.
Our evil genius! It chastises him
Through me, the instrument of his ambition;
And I expect no less, than that Revenge
E'en now is whetting for *my* breast the poignard.
Who sows the serpent's teeth, let him not hope
To reap a joyous harvest. Every crime
Has, in the moment of its perpetration,
Its own avenging angel—dark Misgiving,
An ominous Sinking at the inmost heart.
He can no longer trust me—Then no longer

Can I retreat—so come that which must come.—
Still destiny preserves its due relations,
The heart within us is its absolute
Vicegerent.   [*To* TERTSKY.
        Go, conduct you Gustave Wrangel
To my state-cabinet.—Myself will speak to
The couriers.—And dispatch immediately
A servant for Octavio Piccolomini.

    [*To the* COUNTESS, *who cannot conceal her triumph.*

No exultation!—woman, triumph not!
For jealous are the Powers of Destiny.
Joy premature, and shouts ere victory,
Incroach upon their rights and privileges.
We sow the seed, and they the growth determine.
      [*While he is making his exit the curtain drops.*

ACT V.

SCENE I.—*As in the preceding Act.*

WALLENSTEIN, OCTAVIO PICCOLOMINI.

Wal. [*coming forward in conversation.*] He
    sends me word from Linz, that he lies sick;
But I have sure intelligence, that he
Secretes himself at Frauenberg with Galas.
Secure them both, and send them to me hither.

Remember, thou tak'st on thee the command
Of those same Spanish regiments,—constantly
Make preparation, and be never ready;
And if they urge thee to draw out against me,
Still answer yes, and stand as thou wert fettered.
I know, that it is doing thee a service
To keep thee out of action in this business.
Thou lov'st to linger on in fair appearances;
Steps of extremity are not thy province,
Therefore have I sought out this part for thee.
Thou wilt this time be of most service to me
By thy inertness. The mean time, if fortune
Declare itself on my side, thou wilt know
What is to do.

Enter MAX. PICCOLOMINI.
     Now go, Octavio.
This night must thou be off, take my own horses:
Him here I keep with me—make short farewell—
Trust me, I think we shall all meet again
In joy and thriving fortunes.
 Oct. [*to his son.*]   I shall see you
Yet ere I go.

SCENE II.—WALLENSTEIN, MAX. PICCOLOMINI.

 Max. [*advances to him.*] My General!
 Wal.   That am I no longer, if
Thou styl'st thyself the Emperor's officer.

Max. Then thou wilt leave the army, General?

Wal. I have renounced the service of the Emperor.

Max. And thou wilt leave the army?

Wal.   Rather hope I
To bind it nearer still and faster to me.
                        [*He seats himself.*

Yes, Max., I have delayed to open it to thee,
Even till the hour of acting 'gins to strike.
Youth's fortunate feeling doth seize easily
The absolute right, yea, and a joy it is
To exercise the single apprehension
Where the sums square in proof;
But where it happens, that of two sure evils
One must be taken, where the heart not wholly
Brings itself back from out the strife of duties,
There 'tis a blessing to have no election,
And blank necessity is grace and favour.
—This is now present: do not look behind thee,—
It can no more avail thee. Look thou forwards;
Think not! judge not! prepare thyself to act!
The Court—it hath determined on my ruin,
Therefore I will to be beforehand with them.
We'll join the Swedes—right gallant fellows are they,
And our good friends.
     [*He stops himself, expecting* PICCOLOMINI'S *answer.*

I have ta'en thee by surprise. Answer me not.
I grant thee time to recollect thyself.

> [*He rises, and retires at the back of the stage.* MAX. *remains for a long time motionless, in a trance of excessive anguish. At his first motion* WALLENSTEIN *returns, and places himself before him.*

Max. My General, this day thou makest me
Of age to speak in my own right and person,
For till this day I have been spared the trouble
To find out my own road. Thee have I followed
With most implicit unconditional faith,
Sure of the right path if I followed thee.
To-day, for the first time, dost thou refer
Me to myself, and forcest me to make
Election between thee and my own heart.

Wal. Soft cradled thee thy Fortune till to-day:
Thy duties thou couldst exercise in sport,
Indulge all lovely instincts, act for ever
With undivided heart. It can remain
No longer thus. Like enemies, the roads
Start from each other. Duties strive with duties.
Thou must needs choose thy party in the war
Which is now kindling 'twixt thy friend and him
Who is thy Emperor.

Max. War! is that the name?
War is as frightful as heaven's pestilence.
Yet it is good, is it heaven's will as that is.
Is that a good war, which against the Emperor
Thou wagest with the Emperor's own army?
O God of heaven! what a change is this.

Beseems it me to offer such persuasion
To thee, who like the fixt star of the pole,
Wert all I gazed at on life's trackless ocean?
O! what a rent thou makest in my heart!
The ingrained instinct of old reverence,
The holy habit of obediency,
Must I pluck live asunder from thy name?
Nay, do not turn thy countenance upon me—
It always was as a god looking at me!
Duke Wallenstein, its power is not departed:
The senses still are in thy bonds, although,
Bleeding, the soul hath freed itself.

Wal.   Max., hear me.

Max. O! do it not, I pray thee, do it not!
There is a pure and noble soul within thee,
Knows not of this unblest, unlucky doing.
Thy will is chaste, it is thy fancy only
Which hath polluted thee—and innocence,
It will not let itself be driven away
From that world-awing aspect. Thou wilt not,
Thou canst not, end in this. It would reduce
All human creatures to disloyalty
Against the nobleness of their own nature.
'Twill justify the vulgar misbelief,
Which holdeth nothing noble in free will,
And trusts itself to impotence alone
Made powerful only in an unknown power.

Wal. The world will judge me sternly, I expect it.
Already have I said to my own self

All thou canst say to me. Who but avoids
Th' extreme,—can he by going round avoid it?
But here there is no choice. Yes—I must use
Or suffer violence—so stands the case,
There remains nothing possible but that.

Max. O that is never possible for thee!
'Tis the last desperate resource of those
Cheap souls, to whom their honour, their good name
Is their poor *saving*, their last worthless *Keep*,
Which having staked and lost, they stake themselves
In the mad rage of gaming. Thou art rich,
And glorious; with an unpolluted heart
Thou canst make conquest of whate'er seems highest;
But he, who once hath acted infamy,
Does nothing more in this world.

Wal. [*grasps his hand.*]   Calmly, Max.!
Much that is great and excellent will we
Perform together yet. And if we only
Stand on the height with dignity, 'tis soon
Forgotten, Max., by what road we ascended.
Believe me, many a crown shines spotless now,
That yet was deeply sullied in the winning.
To the evil spirit doth the earth belong,
Not to the good. All, that the powers divine
Send from above, are universal blessings:
Their light rejoices us, their air refreshes,
But never yet was man enriched by them:

In their eternal realm no *property*
Is to be struggled for—all there is general.
The jewel, the all-valued gold we win
From the deceiving Powers, depraved in nature,
That dwell beneath the day and blessed sun-light;
Not without sacrifices are they rendered
Propitious, and there lives no soul on earth
That e'er retired unsullied from their service.

Max. Whate'er is human, to the human being
Do I allow—and to the vehement
And striving spirit readily I pardon
Th' excess of action; but to thee, my General!
Above *all* others make I large concession.
For thou must move a world, and be the master—
He kills thee, who condemns thee to inaction.
So be it then! maintain thee in thy post
By violence. Resist the Emperor,
And if it must be, force with force repel:
I will not praise it, yet I can forgive it.
But not—not to the *traitor*—yes!—the word
Is spoken out——
Not to the traitor can I yield a pardon.
That is no mere excess! that is no error
Of human nature—that is wholly different;
O that is black, black as the pit of hell!
         [WALLENSTEIN *betrays a sudden agitation.*
Thou canst not hear it *named*, and wilt thou *do* it?
O turn back to thy duty. That thou canst,
I hold it certain. Send me to Vienna.
I'll make thy peace for thee with th' Emperor.

He knows thee not. But I do know thee. He
Shall see thee, Duke! with my unclouded eye,
And I bring back his confidence to thee.

    Wal. It is too late. Thou know'st not what
        has happened.

    Max. Were it too late, and were things gone
        so far,
That a crime only could prevent thy fall,
Then—fall! fall honourably, even as thou stood'st,
Lose the command. Go from the stage of war.
Thou canst with splendour do it—do it too
With innocence. Thou hast lived much for others,
At length live thou for thy own self. I follow thee.
My destiny I never part from thine.

    Wal. It is too late! Even now, while thou art
        losing
Thy words, one after the other are the mile-stones
Left fast behind by my post couriers,
Who bear the order on to Prague and Egra.

    [Max. *stands as convulsed, with a gesture and countenance*
        expressing the most intense anguish.

Yield thyself to it. We act as we are forced.
I cannot give assent to my own shame
And ruin. Thou—no—*thou* canst not forsake me!
So let us do, what must be done, with dignity,
With a firm step. What am I doing worse
Than did famed Cæsar at the Rubicon,
When he the legions led against his country,
The which his country had delivered to him?
Had he thrown down the sword, he had been lost,

As I were, if I but disarmed myself.
I trace out something in me of his spirit.
Give me his luck, *that other thing* I'll bear.

> [MAX. *quits him abruptly.* WALLENSTEIN, *startled and overpowered, continues looking after him, and is still in this posture when* TERTSKY *enters.*

SCENE III.—WALLENSTEIN, TERTSKY.

Ter. Max. Piccolomini just left you?
Wal.   Where is Wrangel?
Ter. He is already gone.
Wal.   In such a hurry?
Ter. It is as if the earth had swallowed him.
He had scarce left thee, when I went to seek him.
I wished some words with him—but he was gone.
How, when, and where, could no one tell me. Nay
I half believe it was the devil himself;
A human creature could not so at once
Have vanished.
  Illo. [*enters.*] Is it true that thou wilt send
Octavio?
  Ter. How, Octavio! Whither send him!
  Wal. He goes to Frauenberg, and will lead
          hither
The Spanish and Italian regiments.
  Illo.   No!
Nay, Heaven forbid!
  Wal.   And why should Heaven forbid?
  Illo. Him!—that deceiver! Would'st thou trust
          to him

The soldiery? Him wilt thou let slip from thee,
Now, in the very instant that decides us——

   Ter. Thou wilt not do this!—No! I pray thee,
      no!

   Wal. Ye are whimsical.

   Illo.   O but for this time, Duke,
Yield to our warning! Let him not depart.

   Wal. And why should I not trust him only this
      time,
Who have always trusted him? What, then, has
      happened,
That I should lose my good opinion of him?
In complaisance to your whims, not my own,
I must, forsooth, give up a rooted judgment.
Think not I am a woman. Having trusted him
E'en till to-day, to-day too will I trust him.

   Ter. Must it be he—he only! Send another.

   Wal. It must be he, whom I myself have
      chosen;
He is well fitted for the business. Therefore
I gave it him.

   Illo.   Because he's an Italian—
Therefore is he well fitted for the business.

   Wal. I know you love them not—nor sire nor
      son—
Because that I esteem them, love them—visibly
Esteem them, love them more than you and
      others,
E'en as they merit. Therefore are they eye-
      blights,

Thorns in your foot-path. But your jealousies,
In what affect they me or my concerns?
Are they the worse to me because you hate them?
Love or hate one another as you will,
I leave to each man his own moods and likings;
Yet know the worth of each of you to me.

Illo. Von Questenberg, while he was here, was always
Lurking about with this Octavio.

Wal. It happened with my knowledge and permission.

Illo. I know that secret messengers came to him
From Galas——

Wal.   That's not true.

Illo.   O thou art blind
With thy deep-seeing eyes.

Wal.   Thou wilt not shake
My faith for me—my faith, which founds itself
On the profoundest science. If 'tis false,
Then the whole science of the stars is false.
For know, I have a pledge from fate itself,
That he is the most faithful of my friends.

Illo. Hast thou a pledge, that this pledge is not false?

Wal. There exist moments in the life of man
When he is nearer the great Soul of the world
Than is man's custom, and possesses freely
The power of questioning his destiny:
And such a moment 'twas, when in the night

Before the action in the plains of Lützen,
Leaning against a tree, thoughts crowding thoughts,
I looked out far upon the ominous plain.
My whole life, past and future in this moment
Before my mind's eye glided in procession,
And to the destiny of the next morning
The spirit, filled with anxious presentiment,
Did knit the most removed futurity.
Then said I also to myself, " So many
Dost thou command. They follow all thy stars
And as on some great number set their All
Upon thy single head, and only man
The vessel of thy fortune. Yet a day
Will come, when destiny shall once more scatter
All these in many a several direction:
Few be they who will stand out faithful to thee."
I yearned to know which one was faithfullest
Of all, this camp included. Great Destiny,
Give me a sign! And he shall be the man,
Who, on the approaching morning, comes the first
To meet me with a token of his love:
And thinking this, I fell into a slumber.
Then midmost in the battle was I led
In spirit. Great the pressure and the tumult!
Then was my horse killed under me: I sank:
And over me away all unconcernedly,
Drove horse and rider—and thus trod to pieces
I lay, and panted like a dying man.
Then seized me suddenly a saviour arm;
It was Octavio's—I awoke at once,

'Twas broad day, and *Octavio* stood before me.
"My brother," said he, "do not ride to-day
The dapple, as you're wont; but mount the horse
Which I have chosen for thee. Do it, brother!
In love to me. A strong dream warned me so."
It was the swiftness of this horse that snatched me
From the hot pursuit of Bannier's dragoons.
My cousin rode the dapple on that day,
And never more saw I or horse or rider.

    Illo. That was a chance.

    Wal. [*significantly.*] There's no such thing as
        chance.
In brief, 'tis signed and sealed that this Octavio
Is my good angel—and now no word more.

                          [*He is retiring.*

    Ter. This is my comfort—Max. remains our
        hostage.

    Illo. And he shall never stir from here alive.

    Wal. [*stops and turns himself round.*] Are ye
        not like the women, who for ever
Only recur to their first word, although
One had been talking reason by the hour?
Know, that the human being's thoughts and deeds
Are not, like ocean billows, blindly moved.
The inner world, his microcosmus, is
The deep shaft, out of which they spring eternally.
They grow by certain laws, like the tree's fruit—
No juggling chance can metamorphose them.
Have I the human *kernel* first examined?
Then I know, too, the future will and action.

Scene IV.—*A Chamber in* Piccolomini's *Dwelling-house.*
Octavio Piccolomini, Isolani (*entering*).

Iso. Here am I—Well! who comes yet of the
others?
Oct. [*with an air of mystery.*] But, first, a
word with you, Count Isolani.
Iso. [*with the same air of mystery.*] Will it
explode, ha?—Is the Duke about
To make th' attempt? In me, friend, you may
place
Full confidence.—Nay, put me to the proof.
Oct. That may happen.
Iso. Noble brother, I am
Not one of those men who in words are valiant,
And when it comes to action skulk away.
The Duke has acted t'wards me as a friend.
God knows it is so; and I owe him all——
He may rely on my fidelity.
Oct. That will be seen hereafter.
Iso. Be on your guard,
All think not as I think; and there are many
Who still hold with the Court—yes, and they say
That those stol'n signatures bind them to nothing.
Oct. I am rejoiced to hear it.
Iso. You rejoice!
Oct. That the Emperor has yet such gallant
servants,
And loving friends.

Iso.   Nay, jeer not, I entreat you.
They are no such worthless fellows, I assure you.
  Oct. I am assured already.   God forbid
That I should jest!—In very serious earnest
I am rejoiced to see an honest cause
So strong.
  Iso.   The devil!—what!—why, what means
              this?
Are you not, then——For what, then, am I here?
  Oct. That you may make full declaration,
              whether
You will be called the friend or enemy
Of th' Emperor.
  Iso. [*with an air of defiance.*] That declara-
              tion, friend,
I'll make to him in whom a right is placed
To put that question to me.
  Oct.   Whether, Count,
That right is mine, this paper may instruct you.
  Iso. [*stammering.*] Why,—why—what! This
              is the Emperor's hand and seal!
                                        [*Reads.*
" Whereas the officers collectively
Throughout our army will obey the orders
Of the Lieutenant-General Piccolomini.
As from ourselves."——*Hem!*—Yes! so!—Yes!
              yes!—
I—I give you joy, Lieutenant-General!
  Oct. And you submit you to the order?
  Iso.   I———

But you have taken me so by surprise—
Time for reflection one *must* have——
   Oct.   Two minutes.
   Iso. My God! But then the case is——
   Oct.   Plain and simple.
You must declare you, whether you determine
To act a treason 'gainst your Lord and Sovereign,
Or whether you will serve him faithfully.
   Iso. Treason!—My God!—But who talks then
      of treason?
   Oct. That is the case. The Prince-duke is a
      traitor—
Means to lead over to the enemy
The Emperor's army.—Now, Count!—brief and
      full—
Say, will you break your oath to th' Emperor?
Sell yourself to the enemy?—Say, will you?
   Iso. What mean you? I—I break my oath,
      d'ye say,
To his Imperial Majesty?
Did I say so?—When, when have I said that?
   Oct. You have not said it yet—not yet. This
      instant
I wait to hear, Count, whether you *will* say it.
   Iso. Ay! that delights me now, that you yourself
Bear witness for me that I never said so.
   Oct. And you renounce the Duke then?
   Iso.   If he's planning
Treason—why, treason breaks all bonds asunder.

Oct. And are determined, too, to fight against him?

Iso. He has done me service—but if he's a villain,
Perdition seize him!—All scores are rubbed off.

Oct. I am rejoiced that you're so well disposed.
This night break off in th' utmost secrecy
With all the light-armed troops—it must appear
As came the order from the Duke himself.
At Frauenberg's the place of rendezvous;
There will Count Galas give your further orders.

Iso. It shall be done. But you'll remember me
With th' Emperor—how well disposed you found me.

Oct. I will not fail to mention it honourably.
            [*Exit* Isolani. *A* Servant *enters.*
What, Colonel Butler!—Show him up.

Iso. [*returning.*] Forgive me too my bearish
    ways, old father!   [great
Lord God, how should I know, then, what a
Person I had before me.

Oct.   No excuses!

Iso. I am a merry lad, and if at time
A rash word might escape me 'gainst the Court
Amidst my wine—You know no harm was
    meant.   [*Exit.*

Oct. You need not be uneasy on that score.
That has succeeded. Fortune favour us
With all the others only but as much!

SCENE V.—OCTAVIO PICCOLOMINI, BUTLER.

But. At your command, Lieutenant-General.
Oct. Welcome, as honoured friend and visitor.
But. You do me too much honour.
Oct. [*after both have seated themselves.*] You have not
Returned the advances which I made you yesterday—
Misunderstood them, as mere empty forms.
That wish proceeded from my heart—I was
In earnest with you—for 'tis now a time
In which the honest should unite most closely.
But. 'Tis only the like-minded can unite.
Oct. True! and I name all honest men like-minded.
I never charge a man but with those acts
To which his character deliberately
Impels him; for alas! the violence
Of blind misunderstandings often thrusts
The very best of us from the right track.
You came through Frauenberg. Did the Count Galas
Say nothing to you? Tell me. He's my friend.
But. His words were lost on *me*.
Oct. It grieves me sorely,
To hear it: for his counsel was most wise.
I had myself the like to offer.
But. Spare

Yourself the trouble—me th' embarrassment,
To have deserved so ill your good opinion.

   Oct. The time is precious—let us talk openly.
You know how matters stand here. Wallenstein
Meditates treason—I can tell you further—
He has committed treason; but few hours
Have past, since he a covenant concluded
With th' enemy. The messengers are now
Full on their way to Egra and to Prague.
To-morrow he intends to lead us over
To th' enemy. But he deceives himself;
For prudence wakes—the Emperor has still
Many and faithful friends here, and they stand
In closest union, mighty though unseen.
This manifesto sentences the Duke—
Recalls the obedience of the army from him,
And summons all the loyal, all the honest,
To join and recognize in me their leader.
Choose—will you share with us an honest cause?
Or with the evil share an evil lot.

   But. [*rises.*] His lot is mine.
   Oct.   Is that your last resolve?
   But. It is.
   Oct.   Nay, but bethink you, Colonel Butler!
As yet you have time. Within my faithful breast
That rashly uttered word remains interred.
Recall it, Butler! choose a better party:
You have not chosen the right one.

   But. [*going.*]   Any other
Commands for me, Lieutenant-General?

Oct. See your white hairs ! Recall that word !
But. Farewell !
Oct. What would you draw this good and gallant sword
In such a cause ? Into a curse would you
Transform the gratitude which you have earned
By forty years' fidelity from Austria?
But. [*laughing with bitterness.*] Gratitude from the House of Austria. [*He is going.*
Oct. [*permits him to go as far as the door, then calls after him.*] Butler !
But. What wish you ?
Oct. How was't with the Count ?
But. Count ? what ?
Oct. [*coldly.*] The title that you wished I mean.
But. [*starts in sudden passion.*] Hell and damnation !
Oct. [*coldly.*] You petitioned for it—
And your petition was repelled—Was it so ?
But. Your insolent scoff shall not go by unpunished.
Draw !
Oct. Nay ! your sword to 'ts sheath ! and tell me calmly,
How all that happened. I will not refuse you
Your satisfaction afterwards.—Calmly, Butler !
But. Be the whole world acquainted with the weakness
For which I never can forgive myself.
Lieutenant-General ! Yes—I have ambition.

Ne'er was I able to endure contempt.
It stung me to the quick, that birth and title
Should have more weight than merit has in th'
    army.
I would fain not be meaner than my equal,
So in an evil hour I let myself
Be tempted to that measure—It was folly!
But yet so hard a penance it deserved not.
It might have been refused; but wherefore barb
And venom the refusal with contempt?
Why dash to earth and crush with heaviest
    scorn
The gray-haired man, the faithful Veteran?
Why to the baseness of his parentage
Refer him with such cruel roughness, only
Because he had a weak hour and forgot himself!
But nature gives a sting e'en to the worm
Which wanton power treads on in sport and in-
    sult.

  Oct. You must have been calumniated. Guess
    you
The enemy, who did you this ill service?

  But. Be't who it will—a most low-hearted
    scoundrel.
Some vile court-minion must it be, some Spaniard,
Some young squire of some ancient family,
In whose light I may stand, some envious knave,
Stung to his soul by my fair self-earned honours!

  Oct. But tell me! Did the Duke approve that
    measure?

But. Himself impelled me to it, used his interest
In my behalf with all the warmth of friendship.
 Oct. Ay? Are you sure of that?
 But.   I read the letter.
 Oct. And so did I—but the contents were different.   [BUTLER *is suddenly struck.*
By chance I'm in possession of that letter—
Can leave it to your own eyes to convince you.
       [*He gives him the letter.*
 But. Ha! what is this?
 Oct.   I fear me, Colonel Butler,
An infamous game have they been playing with you.
The Duke, you say, impelled you to this measure?
Now, in this letter talks he in contempt
Concerning you, counsels the Minister
To give sound chastisement to your conceit,
For so he calls it.
  [BUTLER *reads through the letter, his knees tremble, he seizes a chair, and sinks down in it.*
You have no enemy, no persecutor;
There's no one wishes ill to you. Ascribe
The insult you received to the Duke only.
His aim is clear and palpable. He wished
To tear you from your Emperor—he hoped
To gain from your revenge what he well knew
(What your long-tried fidelity convinced him)
He ne'er could dare expect from your calm reason.
A blind tool would he make you, in contempt

Use you, as means of most abandoned ends.
He has gained his point. Too well has he suc-
    ceeded
In luring you away from that good path
On which you had been journeying forty years!
  But. [*his voice trembling.*] Can e'er the Em-
    peror's Majesty forgive me?
  Oct. More than forgive you. He would fain
    compensate
For that affront, and most unmerited grievance
Sustained by a deserving, gallant veteran.
From his free impulse he confirms the present,
Which the Duke made you for a wicked pur-
    pose.
The regiment, which you now command, is yours.

  [BUTLER *attempts to rise, sinks down again. He la-
  bours inwardly with violent emotions; tries to speak,
  and cannot. At length he takes his sword from the belt,
  and offers it to* PICCOLOMINI.

  Oct. What wish you? Recollect yourself,
    friend.
  But.   Take it.
  Oct. But to what purpose? Calm yourself.
  But.   O take it!
I am no longer worthy of this sword.
  Oct. Receive it then anew from my hands—
    and
Wear it with honour for the right cause ever.
  But. —— Perjure myself to such a gracious
    Sovereign!

Oct. You'll make amends.   Quick! break off
  from the Duke!

But. Break off from him!

Oct.   What now? Bethink thyself.

But. [*no longer governing his emotion.*] Only
  break off from him?—He dies! he dies!

Oct. Come after me to Frauenberg, where now
All who are loyal are assembling under
Counts Altringer and Galas.   Many others
I've brought to a remembrance of their duty.
This night be sure, that you escape from Pilsen.

But. [BUTLER *strides up and down in excessive agitation, then steps up to* OCT. *with resolved countenance.*] Count Piccolomini! Dare that man
  speak
Of honour to you, who once broke his troth.

Oct. He who repents so deeply of it, dares.

But. Then leave me here, upon my word of
  honour!

Oct. What's your design?

But.   Leave me and my regiment.

Oct. I have full confidence in you. But tell me
What are you brooding?

But.   That the deed will tell you.
Ask me no more at present.   Trust to me.
Ye may trust safely.   By the living God
Ye give him over not to his good angel!
Farewell.   [*Exit* BUTLER.

Ser. [*enters with a billet.*] A stranger left it
  and is gone.

The Prince-duke's horses wait for you below.
[*Exit* Servant.

Oct. [*reads.*] "Be sure, make haste! Your faithful Isolan."
—O that I had but left this town behind me.
To split upon a rock so near the haven!—
Away! this is no longer a safe place for me!
Where can my son be tarrying?

SCENE VI.—OCTAVIO *and* MAX. PICCOLOMINI.—MAX. *enters in a state of derangement from extreme agitation, his eyes roll wildly, his walk is unsteady, he appears not to observe his father, who stands at a distance, and gazes at him with a countenance expressive of compassion. He paces with long strides through the chamber, then stands still again, and at last throws himself into a chair, staring vacantly at the object directly before him.*

Oct. [*advances to* MAX.] I am going off, my son.
[*Receiving no answer, he takes his hand.*
My son, farewell.
Max. Farewell.
Oct. Thou wilt soon follow me?
Max. I follow thee?
Thy way is crooked—it is not my way.
[OCTAVIO *drops his hand, and starts back.*
O, hadst thou been but simple and sincere,
Ne'er had it come to this—all had stood otherwise
He had not done that foul and horrible deed,
The virtuous had retained their influence o'er him
He had not fallen into the snares of villains.
Wherefore so like a thief, and thief's accomplice

Did'st creep behind him—lurking for thy prey?
O, unblest falsehood! Mother of all evil!
Thou misery-making demon, it is thou
That sink'st us in perdition. Simple truth,
Sustainer of the world, had saved us all!
Father, I will not, I cannot excuse thee!
Wallenstein has deceived me—O, most foully!
But thou hast acted not much better.

Oct.   Son!
My son, ah! I forgive thy agony!

Max. [*rises and contemplates his father with looks of suspicion.*] Was't possible? had'st thou the heart, my father,
Had'st thou the heart to drive it to such lengths,
With cold premeditated purpose? Thou—
Had'st thou the heart, to wish to see him guilty,
Rather than saved? Thou risest by his fall.
Octavio, 'twill not please me.

Oct.   God in heaven!

Max. O woe is me! sure I have changed my nature.
How comes suspicion here—in the free soul?
Hope, confidence, belief, are gone; for all
Lied to me, all what I e'er loved or honoured.
No! No! Not all! She—she yet lives for me,
And she is true, and open as the heavens!
Deceit is everywhere, hypocrisy,
Murder, and poisoning, treason, perjury:
The single holy spot is now our love,
The only unprofaned in human nature.

Oct. Max.!—we will go together. 'Twill be
    better.
Max. What? ere I've taken a last parting leave,
The very last—no, never!
Oct.   Spare thyself
The pang of necessary separation.
Come with me! Come, my son!

                  [*Attempts to take him with him.*

Max. No! as sure as God lives, no!
Oct. [*more urgently.*] Come with me, I com-
    mand thee! I, thy father.
Max. Command me what is human. I stay
    here.
Oct. Max.! in the Emperor's name I bid thee
    come.
Max. No Emperor has power to prescribe
Laws to the heart! and would'st thou wish to
    rob me
Of the sole blessing which my fate has left me,
Her sympathy. Must then a cruel deed
Be done with cruelty? The unalterable
Shall I perform ignobly—steal away,
With stealthy coward flight forsake her? No!
She shall behold my suffering, my sore anguish,
Hear the complaints of the disparted soul,
And weep tears o'er me. Oh! the human race
Have steely souls—but she is an angel.
From the black deadly madness of despair
Will she redeem my soul, and in soft words
Of comfort, plaining, loose this pang of death!

Oct. Thou will not tear thyself away; thou canst not.
O, come, my son! I bid thee save thy virtue.
Max. Squander not thou thy words in vain.
The heart I follow, for I dare trust to it.
Oct. [*trembling and losing all self-command.*]
Max! Max! if that most damned thing could be,
If thou—my son—my own blood—(dare I *think* it?)
Do sell thyself to him, the infamous,
Do stamp this brand upon our noble house,
Then shall the world behold the horrible deed,
And in unnatural combat shall the steel
Of the son trickle with the father's blood.
Max. O hadst thou always better thought of men,
Thou hadst then acted better. Curst suspicion!
Unholy miserable doubt! To him
Nothing on earth remains unwrenched and firm,
Who has no faith.
Oct. And if I trust thy heart,
Will it be always in thy power to follow it?
Max. The heart's voice *thou* hast not o'erpower'd—as little
Will Wallenstein be able to o'erpower it.
Oct. O, Max.! I see thee never more again!
Max. Unworthy of thee wilt thou never see me.
Oct. I go to Frauenberg—the Pappenheimers
I leave thee here, the Lothrings too; Toskana
And Tiefenbach remain here to protect thee.

They love thee, and are faithful to their oath,
And will far rather fall in gallant contest
Than leave their rightful leader, and their honour.
   Max. Rely on this, I either leave my life
In the struggle, or conduct them out of Pilsen.
   Oct. Farewell, my son!
   Max.   Farewell!
   Oct.   How? not one look
Of filial love? No grasp of th' hand at parting?
It is a bloody war, to which we are going,
And the event uncertain and in darkness.
So used we not to part—it was not so!
Is it then true, I have a son no longer?

     [**Max.** *falls into his arms; they hold each for a long time*
       in a speechless embrace, then go away at different sides.]

The Curtain drops.

THE
DEATH OF WALLENSTEIN.

A TRAGEDY IN FIVE ACTS.

DRAMATIS PERSONÆ.

WALLENSTEIN, *Duke of Friedland, Generalissimo of the Imperial Forces in the Thirty Years' War.*
DUCHESS OF FRIEDLAND, *Wife of Wallenstein.*
THEKLA, *her Daughter, Princess of Friedland.*
THE COUNTESS TERTSKY, *Sister of the Duchess.*
LADY NEUBRUNN.
OCTAVIO PICCOLOMINI, *Lieutenant-General.*
MAX. PICCOLOMINI, *his Son, Colonel of a Regiment of Cuirassiers.*
COUNT TERTSKY, *the Commander of several Regiments, and Brother-in-Law of Wallenstein.*
ILLO, *Field-Marshal, Wallenstein's Confidant.*
BUTLER, *an Irishman, Commander of a Regiment of Dragoons.*
GORDON, *Governor of Egra.*
MAJOR GERALDIN.
CAPTAIN DEVEREUX.
CAPTAIN MACDONALD.
NEUMANN, *Captain of Cavalry, Aide-de-Camp to Tertsky.*
SWEDISH CAPTAIN.
SENI.
BURGOMASTER *of Egra.*
ANSPESSADE *of the Curiassiers.*
GROOM OF THE CHAMBER, } *belonging to the Duke.*
A PAGE,
Cuirassiers, Dragoons, Servants.

THE DEATH OF WALLENSTEIN.

ACT I.

SCENE I.—*A Chamber in the House of the* DUCHESS OF FRIEDLAND. COUNTESS TERTSKY, THEKLA, LADY NEUBRUNN. (*The two latter sit at the same table at work.*)

Coun. [*watching them from the opposite side.*]
    So you have nothing, niece, to ask me?
    Nothing?
I have been waiting for a word from you.
And could you then endure in all this time
Not once to speak his name?
    [THEKLA *remaining silent, the* COUNTESS *rises and advances to her.*
              Why comes this?
Perhaps I am already grown superfluous,
And other ways exist, besides through me?
Confess it to me, Thekla! have you seen him?
  Thek. To-day and yesterday I have not seen him.
  Coun. And not heard from him either? Come, be open!

Thek. No syllable.

Coun. And still you are so calm?

Thek. I am.

Coun. May't please you, leave us, Lady Neubrunn!   [*Exit* LADY NEUBRUNN.

SCENE II.—*The* COUNTESS, THEKLA.

Coun. It does not please me, Princess! that he holds
Himself so *still*, exactly at *this* time.

Thek. Exactly at *this* time?

Coun. He now knows all.
'Twere now the moment to declare himself.

Thek. If I'm to understand you, speak less darkly.

Coun. 'Twas for that purpose that I bade her leave us.
Thekla, you are no more a child. Your heart
Is now no more in nonage: for you love,
And boldness dwells with love—that *you* have proved.
Your nature moulds itself upon your father's
More than your mother's spirit. Therefore may you
Hear, what were too much for her fortitude.

Thek. Enough! no further preface, I entreat you.
At once out with it! Be it what it may,

It is not possible that it should torture me
More than this introduction. What have you
To say to me? Tell me the whole and briefly!
   Coun. You'll not be frightened—
   Thek.   Name it, I entreat you.
   Coun. It lies within your power to do your
       father
A weighty service—
   Thek.   Lies within *my* power?
   Coun. Max. Piccolomini loves you. You can
       link him
Indissolubly to your father.
   Thek.   I?
What need of me for that? And is he not
Already linked to him?
   Coun.   He was.
   Thek.   And wherefore
Should he not be so now—not be so always?
   Coun. He cleaves to th' Emperor too.
   Thek.   Not more than duty
And honour may demand of him.
   Coun.   We ask
Proofs of his love, and not proofs of his honour.
Duty and honour!
Those are ambiguous words with many meanings.
You should interpret them for him: his love
Should be the sole definer of his honour.
   Thek. How?
   Coun.   Th' Emperor or you must he re-
       nounce.

Thek. He will accompany my father gladly
In his retirement.   From himself you heard,
How much he wished to lay aside the sword.
　　Coun. He must *not* lay the sword aside, we mean;
He must unsheath it in your father's cause.
　　Thek. He'll spend with gladness and alacrity
His life, his heart's blood in my father's cause,
If shame or injury be intended him.
　　Coun. You will not understand me. Well, hear then!
Your father has fallen off from the Emperor.
And is about to join the enemy
With the whole soldiery—
　　Thek.　　　　　　Alas, my mother!
　　Coun. There needs a great example to draw on
The army after him.   The Piccolomini
Possess the love and reverence of the troops;
They govern all opinions, and wherever
They lead the way, none hesitate to follow.
The son secures the father to our interests—
You've much in your hands at this moment.
　　Thek.　　　　　　　　　　Ah,
My miserable mother! what a death-stroke
Awaits thee!—No!   She never will survive it.
　　Coun. She will accommodate her soul to that
Which is and must be.   I do know your mother.
The far-off future weighs upon her heart
With torture of anxiety; but is it
Unalterably, actually present,

She soon resigns herself, and bears it calmly.
  Thek. O my foreboding bosom! Even now,
E'en now 'tis here, that icy hand of horror!
And my young hope lies shuddering in its grasp;
I knew it well—no sooner had I entered,
A heavy ominous presentiment
Revealed to me, that spirits of death were hovering
Over my happy fortune. But why think I
First of myself? My mother! O my mother!
  Coun. Calm yourself! Break not out in vain
      lamenting!
Preserve you for your father the firm friend,
And for yourself the lover, all will yet
Prove good and fortunate.
  Thek.   Prove *good?* What good?
Must we not part? Part ne'er to meet again?
  Coun. He parts not from you. He can not
      part from you.
  Thek. Alas for his sore anguish! It will rend
His heart asunder.
  Coun.   If indeed he loves you,
His resolution will be speedily taken.
  Thek. His resolution will be speedily taken—
O do not doubt of that! A resolution!
Does there remain one to be *taken?*
  Coun.   Hush!
Collect yourself! I hear your mother coming.
  Thek. How shall I bear to see her?
  Coun.   Collect yourself.

SCENE III.—*To them enter the* DUCHESS.

Duch. [*to the* COUNTESS.] Who was here sister? I heard some one talking,
And passionately too.
   Coun.   Nay! There was no one.
   Duch. I am grown so timorous, every trifling noise
Scatters my spirits, and announces to me
The footstep of some messenger of evil.
And can you tell me, sister, what the event is?
Will he agree to do the Emperor's pleasure,
And send th' horse regiments to the Cardinal?
Tell me, has he dismissed Von Questenberg
With a favourable answer?
   Coun.   No, he has not.
   Duch. Alas! then all is lost! I see it coming,
The worst that can come! Yes, they will depose him;
The accursed business of the Regenspurg diet
Will all be acted o'er again!
   Coun.   No! never!
Make your heart easy, sister, as to that.
   [THEKLA, *in extreme agitation, throws herself upon her Mother, and enfolds her in her arms, weeping.*
   Duch. Yes, my poor child!
Thou too hast lost a most affectionate godmother
In th' Empress. O that stern unbending man!
In this unhappy marriage what have I
Not suffered, not endured. For ev'n as if

I had been linked on to some wheel of fire
That restless, ceaseless, whirls impetuous onward,
I have passed a life of frights and horrors with
  him,
And ever to the brink of some abyss
With dizzy headlong violence he whirls me.
Nay, do not weep, my child! Let not my suf-
  ferings
Presignify unhappiness to thee,
Nor blacken with their shade the *fate* that waits
  thee.
There lives no second Friedland; thou, my child,
Hast not to fear thy mother's destiny.
 Thek. O let us supplicate him, dearest mother!
Quick! quick! here's no abiding place for us.
Here every coming hour broods into life
Some new affrightful monster.
 Duch.   Thou wilt share
An easier, calmer lot, my child! We too,
I and thy father, witnessed happy days.
Still think I with delight of those first years,
When he was making progress with glad effort,
When his ambition was a genial fire,
Not that consuming *flame* which now it is.
The Emperor loved him, trusted him: and all
He undertook could not but be successful.
But since that ill-starred day at Regenspurg,
Which plunged him headlong from his dignity,
A gloomy uncompanionable spirit,
Unsteady and suspicious, has possessed him.

His quiet mind forsook him, and no longer
Did he yield up himself in joy and faith
To his old luck, and individual power;
But thenceforth turned his heart and best affections
All to those cloudy sciences, which never
Have yet made happy him who followed them.
   Coun. You see it, sister! as *your* eyes permit
       you.
But surely this is not the conversation
To pass the time in which we are waiting for him.
You know he will be soon here. Would you
       have him
Find *her* in this condition?
   Duch.   Come, my child!
Come, wipe away thy tears, and show thy father
A cheerful countenance. See, the tie-knot here
Is off—this hair must not hang so dishevelled.
Come, dearest! dry thy tears up. They deform
Thy gentle eye—well now—what was I saying?
Yes, in good truth, this Piccolomini
Is a most noble and deserving gentleman.
   Coun. That is he, sister!
   Thek. [*to the* Countess, *with marks of great oppression of spirits.*] Aunt, you will excuse me?
                                          [*Is going.*
   Coun. But whither? See, your father comes.
   Thek. I cannot see him now.
   Coun.   Nay, but bethink you.
   Thek. Believe me, I cannot sustain his presence.
   Coun. But he will miss you, will ask after you.

Duch. What now? Why is she going?
Coun. She's not well.
Duch. [*anxiously.*] What ails then my beloved child?

[*Both follow the* PRINCESS, *and endeavour to detain her. During this* WALLENSTEIN *appears, engaged in conversation with* ILLO.

SCENE IV.—WALLENSTEIN, ILLO, COUNTESS, DUCHESS, THEKLA.

Wal. All quiet in the camp?
Illo. It is all quiet.
Wal. In a few hours may couriers come from Prague
With tidings, that this capital is ours.
Then we may drop the mask, and to the troops
Assembled in this town make known the measure
And its result together. In such cases
Example does the whole. Whoever is foremost
Still leads the herd. An imitative creature
Is man. The troops at Prague conceive no other,
Than that the Pilsen army has gone through
The forms of homage to us; and in Pilsen
They shall swear fealty to us, because
The example has been given them by Prague.
Butler, you tell me, has declared himself.

Illo. At his own bidding, unsolicited,
He came to offer you himself and regiment.

Wal. I find we must not give implicit credence
To every warning voice that makes itself

Be listened to in th' heart.   To hold us back,
Oft does the lying spirit counterfeit
The voice of truth and inward revelation,
Scattering false oracles.   And thus have I
To intreat forgiveness, for that secretly
I've wrong'd this honourable gallant man,
This Butler: for a feeling, of the which
I am not master, (*fear* I would not call it)
Creeps o'er me instantly, with sense of shuddering,
At his approach, and stops love's joyous motion.
And this same man, against whom I am warned,
This honest man is he, who reaches to me
The first pledge of my fortune.
   Illo.   And doubt not
That his example will win over to you
The best men in the army.
   Wal.   Go and send
Isolani hither.   Send him immediately.
He is under recent obligations to me.
With him will I commence the trial.   Go.
                                        [ILLO *exit*.
   Wal. [*turns himself round to the females.*]   Lo,
     there the mother with the darling daughter!
For once we'll have an interval of rest—
Come! my heart yearns to live a cloudless hour
In the beloved circle of my family.
   Coun. 'Tis long since we've been thus together,
     brother.
   Wal. [*to the* COUNTESS *aside.*]   Can she sustain
     the news?   Is she prepared?

Coun. Not yet.
Wal. Come here, my sweet girl! Seat thee by
    me,
For there is a good spirit on thy lips.
Thy mother praised to me thy ready skill:
She says a voice of melody dwells in thee,
Which doth enchant the soul. Now such a voice
Will drive away from me the evil demon
That beats his black wings close above my head.
    Duch. Where is thy lute, my daughter? Let
    thy father
Hear some small trial of thy skill.
    Thek.   My mother!
I—
    Duch. Trembling? Come, collect thyself. Go,
    cheer
Thy father.
    Thek.   O my mother! I—I cannot.
    Coun. How, what is that, niece?
    Thek. [*to the* COUNTESS.] O spare me—sing—
    now—in this sore anxiety
Of the o'erburthened soul—to sing to *him*,
Who is thrusting, even now, my mother headlong
Into her grave!
    Duch.   How, Thekla? Humoursome?
What! shall thy father have expressed a wish
In vain?
    Coun. Here is the lute.
    Thek.   My God! how can I—
    [*The orchestra plays. During the ritornello* THEKLA

expresses in her gestures and countenance the struggle of her feelings: and at the moment that she should begin to sing, contracts herself together, as one shuddering, throws the instrument down, and retires abruptly.]

Duch. My child! O she is ill—
Wal. What ails the maiden?
Say, is she often so?
Coun. Since then herself
Has now betrayed it, I too must no longer
Conceal it.
Wal. What?
Coun. She loves him!
Wal. Loves him! Whom?
Coun. Max. does she love! Max. Piccolomini.
Hast thou ne'er noticed it? Nor yet my sister?
Duch. Was it this that lay so heavy on her
    heart?
God's blessing on thee, my sweet child! Thou
    needest
Never take shame upon thee for thy choice.
Coun. This journey,—if 'twere not thy aim,
    ascribe it
To thine own self. Thou should'st have chosen
    another
To have attended her.
Wal. And does he know it?
Coun. Yes, and he hopes to win her.
Wal. Hopes to win her!
Is the boy mad?

Coun. Well—hear it from themselves.
Wal. He thinks to carry off Duke Friedland's
daughter!
Ay?—The thought pleases me.
The young man has no grovelling spirit.
Coun. Since
Such and such constant favour you have shown
him——
Wal. He chooses finally to be my heir.
And true it is, I love the youth; yea, honour him.
But must he therefore be my daughter's husband!
Is it daughters only? Is it only children
That we must show our favour by?
Duch. His noble disposition and his manners—
Wal. Win him my heart, but not my daughter.
Duch. Then
His rank, his ancestors—
Wal. Ancestors! What?
He is a subject, and my son-in-law
I will seek out upon the thrones of Europe.
Duch. O dearest Albrecht! Climb we not too
high,
Lest we should fall too low.
Wal. What? have I paid
A price so heavy to ascend this eminence,
And jut out high above the common herd,
Only to close the mighty part I play
In life's great drama, with a common kinsman?
Have I for this— [*Stops suddenly, repressing himself.*
She is the only thing

That will remain behind of me on earth;
And I will see a crown around her head,
Or die in the attempt to place it there.
I hazard all—all! and for this alone,
To lift her into greatness—
Yea, in this moment, in the which we are speaking— [*He recollects himself.*
And I must now, like a soft-hearted father,
Couple together in good peasant fashion
The pair, that chance to suit each other's liking—
And I must do it now, even now, when I
Am stretching out the wreath that is to twine
My full accomplished work—no! she is the jewel,
Which I have treasured long, my last, my noblest,
And 'tis my purpose not to let her from me
For less than a king's sceptre.

Duch. O my husband!
You're ever building, building to the clouds,
Still building higher, and still higher building,
And ne'er reflect, that the poor narrow basis
Cannot sustain the giddy tottering column.

Wal. [*to the* COUNTESS.] Have you announced the place of residence
Which I have destined for her?

Coun. No! not yet.
'Twere better you yourself disclosed it to her.

Duch. How? Do we not return to Karn then?
Wal. No.
Duch. And to no other of your lands or seats?
Wal. You would not be secure there.

Duch.   Not secure
In the Emperor's realms, beneath the Emperor's
Protection?
 Wal. Friedland's wife may be permitted
No longer to hope *that*.
 Duch.   O God in heaven!
And have you brought it even to this?
 Wal.   In Holland
You'll find protection.
 Duch.   In a Lutheran country?
What? And you send us into Lutheran countries?
  Wal. Duke Franz of Lauenburg conducts you
    thither.
 Duch. Duke Franz of Lauenburg?
The ally of Sweden, the Emperor's enemy.
  Wal. The Emperor's enemies are mine no
    longer.
 Duch. [*casting a look of terror on the* Duke
and the Countess.] Is it then true? It is. You
    are degraded?
Deposed from the command? O God in heaven!
 Coun. [*aside to the* Duke.] Leave her in this
    belief. Thou seest she cannot
Support the real truth.

 Scene V.—*To them enter* Count Tertsky.

 Coun.   —Tertsky,
What ails him? What an image of affright!
He looks as he had seen a ghost.

Ter. [*leading* WALLENSTEIN *aside.*] Is it thy
  command that all the Croats—
Wal.   Mine!
Ter. We are betrayed.
Wal.   What?
Ter.   They are off! This night
The Jägers likewise—all the villages
In the whole round are empty.
 Wal.   Isolani?
 Ter. Him thou hast sent away. Yes, surely.
 Wal.   I?
 Ter. No! Hast thou not sent him off? Nor
  Deodate?
They are vanished both of them.

   SCENE VI.—*To them enter* ILLO.

 Illo. Has Tertsky told thee?
 Ter.   He knows all.
 Illo.   And likewise
That Esterhatzy, Goetz, Maradas, Kaunitz,
Kolatto, Palfi, have forsaken thee?
 Ter. Damnation!
 Wal. [*winks at them.*] Hush!
 Coun. [*who has been watching them anxiously
from the distance, and now advances to them.*]
Tertsky! Heaven! What is it? What has hap-
  pened?
 Wal. [*scarcely suppressing his emotions.*] No-
  thing! let us be gone!

Ter. [*following him.*] Theresa, it is nothing.
Coun. [*holding him back.*] Nothing? Do I not
    see, that all the life-blood
Has left your cheeks—look you not like a ghost?
That even my brother but affects a calmness?
Page. [*enters.*] An Aide-de-Camp inquires
    for the Count Tertsky.
              [TERTSKY *follows the* Page.
Wal. Go, hear his business.
[*To* ILLO.]   This could not have happened
So unsuspected without mutiny.
Who was on guard at the gates?
Illo.   'Twas Tiefenbach.
Wal. Let Tiefenbach leave guard without delay,
And Tertsky's grenadiers relieve him.
                  [ILLO *is going.*
                  Stop!
Hast thou heard aught of Butler?
Ill.   Him I met.
He will be here himself immediately.
Butler remains unshaken.
         [ILLO *exit.* WALLENSTEIN *is following him.*
Coun. Let him not leave thee, sister! go, detain
    him!
There's some misfortune.
Duch. [*clinging to him.*] Gracious heaven!
    What is it?
Wal. Be tranquil! leave me, sister! dearest
    wife!
We are in camp, and this is nought unusual;

Here storm and sunshine follow one another
With rapid interchanges. These fierce spirits
Champ the curb angrily, and never yet
Did quiet bless the temples of the leader.
If I am to stay, go you. The plaints of women
Ill suit the scene where men must act.
      [*He is going :* TERTSKY *returns.*

Ter. Remain here. From this window must
  we see it.
Wal. [*to the* COUNTESS.] Sister, retire !
Coun.   No—never.
Wal.   'Tis my will.
Ter. [*leads the* COUNTESS *aside, and drawing her attention to the* DUCHESS.] Theresa !
Duch. Sister, come ! since he commands it.

  SCENE VII.—WALLENSTEIN, TERTSKY.

Wal. [*stepping to the window.*] What now,
  then ?
Ter. There are strange movements among all
  the troops,
And no one knows the cause. Mysteriously,
With gloomy silentness, the several corps
Marshal themselves, each under its own banners.
Tiefenbach's corps makes threatening movements;
  only
The Pappenheimers still remain aloof
In their own quarters, and let no one enter.
 Wal. Does Piccolomini appear among them ?

Ter. We are seeking him: he is nowhere to be
    met with.
Wal. What did the Aide-de-Camp deliver to
    you?
Ter. My regiments had dispatched him; yet
    once more
They swear fidelity to thee, and wait
The shout for onset, all prepared, and eager.
Wal. But whence arose this larum in the
    camp?
It should have been kept secret from the army,
Till fortune had decided for us at Prague.
Ter. O that thou hadst believed me! Yester
    evening
Did we conjure thee not to let that skulker,
That Fox, Octavio, pass the gates of Pilsen.
Thou gav'st him thy own horses to flee from thee.
Wal. The old tune still! Now, once for all,
    no more
Of this suspicion—it is doting folly.
Ter. Thou didst confide in Isolani too;
And lo! he was the first that did desert thee.
Wal. It was but yesterday I rescued him
From abject wretchedness. Let that go by.
I never reckon'd yet on gratitude.
And wherein doth he wrong in going from me?
He follows still the god whom all his life
He has worshipped at the gaming table. With
My fortune, and my seeming destiny,
He made the bond, and broke it not with me.

I am but the ship in which his hopes were stowed,
And with the which well-pleased and confident
He traversed the open sea; now he beholds it
In imminent jeopardy among the coast-rocks,
And hurries to preserve his wares.   As light
As the free bird from the hospitable twig
Where it had nested, he flies off from me:
No human tie is snapped betwixt us two.
Yea, he deserves to find himself deceived,
Who seeks a heart in the unthinking man,
Like shadows on a stream, the forms of life
Impress their characters on the smooth forehead,
Nought sinks into the bosom's silent depth:
Quick sensibility of pain and pleasure
Moves the light fluids lightly; but no soul
Warmeth the inner frame.

Ter.   Yet, would I rather
Trust the smooth brow than that deep furrowed
    one.

SCENE VIII.—WALLENSTEIN, TERTSKY, ILLO, *who enters agitated with rage.*

Illo. Treason and mutiny!
Ter.   And what further now?
Illo. Tiefenbach's soldiers, when I gave the
    orders
To go off guard—Mutinous villains!
Ter.   Well!
Wal. What followed?

Illo.   They refused obedience to them.

Ter. Fire on them instantly! Give out the order.

Wal. Gently! what cause did they assign?

Illo.   No other
They said, had right to issue orders but
Lieutenant-General *Piccolomini*.

Wal. [*in convulsion of agony.*] What? How is that?

Illo. He takes that office on him by commission,
Under sign-manual of the emperor.

Ter. From th' Emperor—hear'st thou, Duke?

Illo.   At his incitement
The Generals made that stealthy flight—

Ter.   Duke! hearest thou?

Illo. Caraffa too and Montecuculi,
Are missing, with six other Generals,
All whom he had induced to follow him.
This plot he has long had in writing by him
From the Emperor; but 'twas finally concluded
With all the detail of the operation
Some days ago with the Envoy Questenberg.

[WALLENSTEIN *sinks down into a chair and covers his face.*

Ter. O hadst thou but believed me!

SCENE IX.—*To them enter the* COUNTESS.

Coun.   This suspense,
This horrid fear—I can no longer bear it.
For heaven's sake, tell me, what has taken place.

Illo. The regiments are all falling off from us.
Ter. Octavio Piccolomini is a traitor.
Coun. O my foreboding!
[*Rushes out of the room.*

Ter. Hadst thou but believed me!
Now seest thou how the stars have lied to thee.
Wal. The stars lie not; but we have here a work
Wrought counter to the stars and destiny.
The science is still honest: this false heart
Forces a lie on the truth-telling heaven.
On a divine law divination rests;
Where nature deviates from that law, and stumbles
Out of her limits, there all science errs.
True, I did not suspect! Were it superstition
Never by such suspicion t' have affronted
The human form, O may that time ne'er come
In which I shame me of the infirmity.
The wildest savage drinks not with the victim,
Into whose breast he means to plunge the sword.
This, this, Octavio, was no hero's deed:
'Twas not thy prudence that did conquer mine;
A bad heart triumphed o'er an honest one.
No shield received the assassin stroke; thou plungest
Thy weapon on an unprotected breast—
Against such weapons I am but a child.

THE DEATH OF WALLENSTEIN.

Scene X.—*To these enter* Butler.

Ter. [*meeting him.*] O look there! Butler! Here we've still a friend!

Wal. [*meets him with outspread arms, and embraces him with warmth.*] Come to my heart, old comrade! Not the sun
Looks out upon us more revivingly
In the earliest month of spring,
Than a friend's countenance in such an hour.

But. My General: I come—

Wal. [*leaning on* Butler's *shoulders.*] Know'st thou already?
That old man has betrayed me to the Emperor.
What say'st thou? Thirty years have we together
Lived out, and held out, sharing joy and hardship.
We have slept in one camp-bed, drunk from one glass,
One morsel shared! I leaned myself on *him*,
As now I lean me on *thy* faithful shoulder.
And now in the very moment, when, all love,
All confidence, my bosom beat to his,
He sees and takes the advantage, stabs the knife
Slowly into my heart.

[*He hides his face on* Butler's *breast.*

But. Forget the false one.
What is your present purpose?

Wal. Well remembered!

Courage my soul! I am still rich in friends,
Still loved by Destiny; for in the moment,
That it unmasks the plotting hypocrite,
It sends and proves to me one *faithful* heart.
Of the hypocrite no more! Think not, his loss
Was that which struck the pang: O no! his treason
Is that which strikes this pang! No more of him!
Dear to my heart and honoured were they both,
And the young man—yes—he *did* truly love me,
He—he—has not deceived me. But enough,
Enough of this—Swift counsel now beseems us.
The courier, whom Count Kinsky sent from Prague,
I expect him every moment: and whatever
He may bring with him, we must take good care
To keep it from the mutineers. Quick, then!
Dispatch some messenger you can rely on
To meet him, and conduct him to me. [ILLO *is going.*

But. [*detaining him.*] My General, whom expect you then?

Wal.   The courier
Who brings me word of the event at Prague.

But. [*hesitating.*] Hem!

Wal.   And what now?

But.   You do not know it?

Wal.   Well?

But. From what that larum in the camp arose?

Wal. From what?

But.   That courier—

Wal. [*with eager expectation.*] Well?
But.   Is already here.
Ter. and Illo. [*at the same time.*] Already here?
Wal.   My courier?
But.   For some hours.
Wal. And I not know it?
But.   The sentinels detain him
In custody.
Illo. [*stamping with his foot.*] Damnation!
But.   And his letter
Was broken open, and is circulated
Through the whole camp.
Wal.   You know what it contains?
But. Question me not.
Ter.   Illo! alas for us.
Wal. Hide nothing from me—I can hear the worst.
Prague then is lost. It is. Confess it freely.
But. Yes! Prague *is* lost. And all the several regiments
At Budweiss, Tabor, Brannau, Konigingratz,
At Brun and Znaym, have forsaken you,
And ta'en the oaths of fealty anew
To the Emperor. Yourself, with Kinsky, Tertsky,
And Illo, have been sentenced.

[TERTSKY *and* ILLO *express alarm and fury.* WAL-
 LENSTEIN *remains firm and collected.*

Wal.   'Tis decided!
'Tis well! I have received a sudden cure
From all the pangs of doubt; with steady stream

Once more my life-blood flows! My soul's secure!
In the night only Friedland's stars can beam.
Lingering irresolute, with fitful fears
I drew the sword—'twas with an inward strife,
While yet the choice was mine. The murderous
    knife
Is lifted for my heart! Doubt disappears!
I fight now for my head and for my life.

        [*Exit* WALLENSTEIN; *the others follow him.*

SCENE XI.—COUNTESS TERTSKY (*enters from a side Room.*)

I can endure no longer. No! [*Looks around her.*
                    Where are they!
No one is here. They leave me all alone,
Alone in this sore anguish of suspense.
And I must wear the outward show of calmness
Before my sister, and shut in within me
The pangs and agonies of my crowded bosom.
It is not to be borne.—If all should fail;
If—if he must go over to the Swedes,
An empty-handed fugitive, and not
As an ally, a covenanted equal,
A proud commander with his army following;
If we must wander on from land to land,
Like the Count Palatine, of fallen greatness
An ignominious monument—But no!
That day I will not see! And could himself
Endure to sink so low, I would not bear
To see him so low sunken.

SCENE XII.—COUNTESS, DUCHESS, THEKLA.

Thek. [*endeavouring to hold back the* DUCHESS.]
 Dear mother, do stay here!
Duch.   No! Here is yet
Some frightful mystery that is hidden from me.
Why does my sister shun me? Don't I see her
Full of suspense and anguish roam about
From room to room?—Art thou not full of terror?
And what import these silent nods and gestures
Which stealthwise thou exchangest with her?
 Thek.   Nothing:
Nothing dear mother!
 Duch. [*to the* COUNTESS.] Sister, I will know.
 Coun. What boots it new to hide it from her?
  Sooner
Or later she *must* learn to hear and bear it.
'Tis not the time now to indulge infirmity;—
Courage beseems us now, a heart collected,
And exercise and previous discipline
Of fortitude. One word and over with it!
Sister you are deluded. You believe
The Duke has been deposed—The Duke is not
Deposed—he is——
 Thek. [*going to the* COUNTESS.] What? do you
  wish to kill her?
 Coun. The Duke is——
 Thek. [*throwing her arms round her mother.*] O
  stand firm! stand firm, my mother!
 Coun. Revolted is the Duke, he is preparing

To join the enemy, the army leave him,
And all has failed.

> [*During these words the* DUCHESS *totters, and falls in a faintiny fit into the arms of her daughter. While* THEKLA *is calling for help, the Curtain drops.*

ACT II.

SCENE I.—*A spacious Room in the* DUKE OF FRIEDLAND'S *Palace.*

Wal. [*in armour.*] Thou hast gained thy
   point, Octavio! Once more am I
Almost as friendless as at Regenspurg.
There I had nothing left me, but myself—
But what one man can do, you have now experience.
The twigs have you hewed off, and here I stand
A leafless trunk. But in the sap within
Lives the creating power, and a new world
May sprout forth from it. Once already have I
Proved myself worth an army to you—I alone!
Before the Swedish strength your troops had
   melted;
Beside the Lech sank Tilly, your last hope;
Into Bavaria, like a winter torrent,
Did that Gustavus pour, and at Vienna
In his own palace did the Emperor tremble.
Soldiers were scarce, for still the multitude
Follow the luck; all eyes were turned on me,

Their helper in distress; the Emperor's pride
Bowed itself down before the man he had injured.
'Twas I must rise, and with creative word
Assemble forces in the desolate camps.
I did it. Like a god of war, my name [and, lo!
Went through the world. The drum was beat—
The plough, the workshop is forsaken, all
Swarm to the old familiar long-loved banners;
And as the wood-choir rich in melody
Assemble quick around the bird of wonder,
When first his throat swells with his magic song,
So did the warlike youth of Germany
Crowd in around the image of my eagle.
I feel myself the being that I was.
It is the soul that builds itself a body,
And Friedland's camp will not remain unfilled.
Lead then your thousands out to meet me—true!
They are accustomed under me to conquer,
But not against me. If the head and limbs
Separate from each other, 'twill be soon
Made manifest, in which the soul abode.

[ILLO *and* TERTSKY *enter.*

Courage, friends! Courage! We are still unvan-
    quished;
I feel my footing firm; five regiments, Tertsky,
Are still our own, and Butler's gallant troops;
And a host of sixteen thousand Swedes to-morrow.
I was not stronger, when nine years ago
I marched forth, with glad heart and high of hope,
To conquer Germany for the Emperor.

Scene II.—Wallenstein, Illo, Tertsky. (*To them enter* Neumann, *who leads* Tertsky *aside, and talks with him.*)

Ter. What do they want?
Wal. What now?
Ter. Ten Cuirassiers
From Pappenheim request leave to address you
In the name of the regiment.
Wal. [*hastily to* Neumann.] Let them enter.
[*Exit* Neumann.
This
May end in something. Mark you. They are still
Doubtful, and may be won.

Scene III.—Wallenstein, Tertsky, Illo, *ten* Cuirassiers, (*led by an* Anspessade,* *march up and arrange themselves, after the word of command, in one front before the* Duke, *and make their obeisance. He takes his hat off, and immediately covers himself again.*)

Ans. Halt! Front! Present!
Wal. [*after he has run through them with his eye, to the* Anspessade.] I know thee well. Thou art of Brüggin in Flanders:
Thy name is Mercy.
Ans. Henry Mercy.

* Anspessade, in German, Gefreiter, a soldier inferior to a corporal, but above the sentinels. The German name implies that he is exempt from mounting guard.

Wal. Thou wert cut off on the march, surrounded by the Hessians, and didst fight thy way with a hundred and eighty men through their thousand.

Ans. 'Twas even so, General!

Wal. What reward hadst thou for this gallant exploit?

Ans. That which I asked for: the honour to serve in this corps.

Wal. [*turning to a second.*] Thou wert among the volunteers that seized and made booty of the Swedish battery at Altenburg.

2nd Cui. Yes, General!

Wal. I forget no one with whom I have exchanged words. [*A pause.*] Who sends you?

Ans. Your noble regiment, the Cuirassiers of Piccolomini.

Wal. Why does not your colonel deliver in your request, according to the custom of service?

Ans. Because we would first know *whom* we serve.

Wal. Begin your address.

Ans. [*giving the word of command.*] Shoulder your arms!

Wal. [*turning to a third.*] Thy name is Risbeck, Cologne is thy birth-place.

3rd Cui. Risbeck of Cologne.

Wal. It was thou that broughtest in the Swedish colonel, Diebald, prisoner, in the camp at Nuremberg.

3rd Cui. It was not I, General!

Wal. Perfectly right! It was thy elder brother: thou hadst a younger brother too: Where did he stay?

3rd Cui. He is stationed at Olmutz with the Imperial army.

Wal. [*to the* Anspessade.] Now then—begin.

Ans. There came to hand a letter from the Emperor commanding us——

Wal. [*interrupting him.*] Who chose you?

Ans.   Every company
Drew its own man by lot.

Wal.   Now! to the business.

Ans. There came to hand a letter from the Emperor commanding us collectively, from thee
All duties of obedience to withdraw,
Because thou wert an enemy and traitor.

Wal. And what did you determine?

Ans.   All our comrades
At Brannau, Budweiss, Prague and Olmutz, have
Obeyed already, and the regiments here,
Tiefenbach and Toscana, instantly
Did follow their example. But—but we
Do not believe that thou'rt an enemy
And traitor to thy country, hold it merely
For lie and trick, and a trumped up Spanish story!
          [*With warmth.*
Thyself shalt tell us what thy purpose is,
For we have found thee still sincere and true:
No mouth shall interpose itself betwixt

The gallant General and the gallant troops.
 Wal. Therein I recognize my Pappenheimers.
 Ans. And this proposal makes thy regiment to
  thee:
Is it thy purpose merely to preserve
In thy own hands this military sceptre,
Which so becomes thee, which the Emperor
Made over to thee by a covenant?
Is it thy purpose merely to remain
Supreme commander of the Austrian armies?—
We will stand by thee, General! and guarantee
Thy honest rights against all opposition.
And should it chance, that all the other regiments
Turn from thee, by ourselves will we stand forth
Thy faithful soldiers, and, as is our duty,
Far rather let ourselves be cut to pieces,
Than suffer thee to fall. But if it be
As the Emperor's letter says, if it be true,
That thou in traitorous wise wilt lead us over
To the enemy, which God in heaven forbid!
Then we too will forsake thee, and obey
That letter——
 Wal.   Hear me, children!
 Ans.   Yes, or no!
There needs no other answer.
 Wal.   Yield attention.
You're men of sense, examine for yourselves;
Ye think, and do not follow with the herd:
And therefore have I always shown you honour
Above all others, suffered you to reason;

Have treated you as free men, and my orders
Were but the echoes of your prior suffrage.—
  Ans. Most fair and noble has thy conduct been
To us, my General! With thy confidence
Thou hast honoured us, and shown us grace and
  favour
Beyond all other regiments; and thou seest
We follow not the common herd. We will
Stand by thee faithfully. Speak but one word—
Thy word shall satisfy us, that it is not
A treason which thou meditatest—that
Thou meanest not to lead the army over
To the enemy; nor e'er betray thy country.
  Wal. Me, me are they betraying. The Emperor
Hath sacrificed me to my enemies,
And I must fall, unless my gallant troops
Will rescue me. See! I confide in you.
And be your hearts my stronghold! At this breast
The aim is taken, at this hoary head.
This is your Spanish gratitude, this is our
Requital for that murderous fight at Lutzen!
For this we threw the naked breast against
The halbert, made for this the frozen earth
Our bed, and the hard stone our pillow! never
  stream
Too rapid for us, nor wood too impervious:
With cheerful spirit we pursued that Mansfeld
Through all the turns and windings of his flight;
Yea, our whole life was but one restless march;
And homeless, as the stirring wind, we travelled

O'er the war-wasted earth. And now, even now,
That we have well nigh finished the hard toil,
The unthankful, the curse-laden toil of weapons,
With faithful indefatigable arm
Have rolled the heavy war-load up the hill,
Behold! this boy of the Emperor's bears away
The honours of the peace, an easy prize!
He'll weave, forsooth, into his flaxen locks
The olive branch, the hard-earned ornament
Of this gray head, grown gray beneath the helmet.
   Ans. That shall he not, while we can hinder it!
No one, but thou, who hast conducted it
With fame, shall end this war, this frightful war.
Thou led'st us out into the bloody field
Of death, thou and no other shalt conduct us home,
Rejoicing to the lovely plains of peace—
Shalt share with us the fruits of the long toil—
   Wal. What? Think you then at length in late
       old age
To enjoy the fruits of toil? Believe it not.
Never, no never, will you see the end
Of the contest! you and me, and all of us,
This war will swallow up! War, war, not peace,
Is Austria's wish; and therefore, because I
Endeavoured after peace, therefore I fall.
For what cares Austria, how long the war
Wears out the armies and lays waste the world?
She will but wax and grow amid the ruin,
And still win new domains.
   [*The* Cuirassiers *express agitation by their gestures.*

                        Ye're moved—I see
A noble rage flash from your eyes, ye warriors!
Oh that my spirit might possess you now
Daring as once it led you to the battle!
Ye would stand by me with your veteran arms,
Protect me in my rights; and this is noble!
But think not that *you* can accomplish it,
Your scanty number! to no purpose will you
Have sacrificed you for your General. [*Confidentially.*
No! let us tread securely, seek for friends;
The Swedes have proffered us assistance, let us
Wear for a while the appearance of good will,
And use them for your profit, till we both
Carry the fate of Europe in our hands,
And from our camp to the glad jubilant world
Lead Peace forth with the garland on her head!

   Ans. 'Tis then but mere appearances which thou
Dost put on with the Swede? Thou'lt not betray
The Emperor? Wilt not turn us into Swedes?
This is the only thing which we desire
To learn from thee.

   Wal.   What care I for the Swedes?
I hate them as I hate the pit of hell,
And under Providence I trust right soon
To chase them to their homes across their Baltic.
My cares are only for the whole: I have
A heart—it bleeds within me for the miseries
And piteous groaning of my fellow Germans.
Ye are but common men, but yet ye think
With minds not common; ye appear to me

Worthy before all others, that I whisper ye
A little word or two in confidence!
See now! already for full fifteen years
The war-torch has continued burning, yet
No rest, no pause of conflict. Swede and German,
Papist and Lutheran! neither will give way
To the other, every hand's against the other.
Each one is party, and no one a judge.
Where shall this end? Where's he that will
        unravel
This tangle, ever tangling more and more.
It must be cut asunder.
I feel that I am the man of destiny,
And trust, with your assistance, to accomplish it.

    Scene IV.—*To these enter* Butler.

But. [*passionately.*] General! This is not right!
Wal.   What is not right?
But. It must needs injure us with all honest men.
Wal. But what?
But.   It is an open proclamation
Of insurrection.
Wal.   Well, well—but what is it?
But. Count Tertsky's regiments tear the Im-
    perial Eagle
From off the banners, and instead of it,
Have reared aloft thy arms.
   Ans. [*abruptly to the* Cuirassiers.] Right
      about! March!

Wal. Cursed be this counsel, and accursed
 who gave it!
      [*To the* Curassiers, *who are retiring.*
Halt, children, halt! There's some mistake in
 this;
Hark!—I will punish it severely. Stop!
They do not hear. [*to* Illo.] Go after them,
 assure them,
And bring them back to me, cost what it may.
      [Illo *hurries out.*
This hurls us headlong. Butler! Butler!
You are my evil genius, wherefore must you
Announce it in their presence? It was all
In a fair way. They were half won, those mad-
 men
With their improvident over-readiness:——
A cruel game is Fortune playing with me.
The zeal of friends it is that razes me,
And not the hate of enemies.

Scene V.—*To these enter the* Duchess, *who rushes into the Chamber.* Thekla *and the* Countess *follow her.*

Duch.   O, Albrecht!
What hast thou done?
 Wal.   And now comes this beside.
 Coun. Forgive me, brother! It was not in
 my power.
They know all.

Duch. What hast thou done?

Coun. [*to* TERTSKY.] Is there no hope? Is all lost utterly?

Ter. All lost. No hope. Prague in the Emperor's hands,
The soldiery have ta'en their oaths anew.

Coun. That lurking hypocrite, Octavio!
Count Max. is off too?

Ter. Where can *he* be? He's
Gone over to the Emperor with his father.

[THEKLA *rushes out into the arms of her mother, hiding her face in her bosom.*

Duch. [*enfolding her in her arms.*] Unhappy child! and more unhappy mother!

Wal. [*aside to* TERTSKY.] Quick! Let a carriage stand in readiness
In the court behind the palace. Scherfenberg
Be their attendant; he is faithful to us;
To Egra he'll conduct them, and we follow.

[*To* ILLO, *who returns.*

Thou hast not brought them back?

Illo. Hear'st thou the uproar?
The whole corps of the Pappenheimers is
Drawn out: the younger Piccolomini,
Their Colonel, they require; for they affirm,
That he is in the palace here, a prisoner;
And if thou dost not instantly deliver him,
They will find means to free him with the sword.

[*All stand amazed.*

Ter. What shall we make of this?

Wal. Said I not so?
O my prophetic heart! he is still here.
He has not betrayed me—he could not betray me.
I never doubted of it.
　Coun. If he be
Still here, then all goes well; for I know what
　　　　　　　　　　　　[*Embracing* THEKLA.
Will keep him here for ever.
　Ter. It can't be.
His father has betrayed us, is gone over
To the Emperor—the son could not have ventured
To stay behind.
　Thek. [*her eye fixed on the door.*] There he is!

SCENE VI.—*To these enter* MAX. PICCOLOMINI.

Max. Yes! here he is! I can endure no longer
To creep on tiptoe round this house, and lurk
In ambush for a favourable moment.
This loitering, this suspense exceeds my powers.
　[*Advancing to* THEKLA, *who has thrown herself into her
　　mother's arms.*
Turn not thine eyes away. O look upon me!
Confess it freely before all. Fear no one.
Let who will hear that we both love each other.
Wherefore continue to conceal it? Secrecy
Is for the happy—misery, hopeless misery,
Needeth no veil! Beneath a thousand suns
It dares act openly.
　[*He observes the* COUNTESS *looking on* THEKLA *with
　　expressions of triumph.*

No, lady! No!
Expect not, hope it not. I am not come
To stay: to bid farewell, farewell for ever,
For this I come! 'Tis over! I must leave thee!
Thekla, I must—*must* leave thee! Yet thy hatred
Let me not take with me. I pray thee, grant me
One look of sympathy, only one look.
Say that thou dost not hate me. Say it to me,
    Thekla!   [*Grasps her hand.*
O God! I cannot leave this spot—I cannot—
Cannot let go this hand. O tell me, Thekla!
That thou dost suffer with me, art convinced
That I can not act otherwise.

> [THEKLA, *avoiding his look, points with her hand to her father.* MAX. *turns round to the* DUKE, *whom he had not till then perceived.*

Thou here? It was not thou, whom here I sought.
I trusted never more to have beheld thee.
My business is with her alone. Here will I
Receive a full acquittal from this heart—
For any other I am no more concerned.
  Wal. Think'st thou, that fool-like, I shall let
    thee go,
And act the mock-magnanimous with thee?
Thy father is become a villain to me;
I hold thee for his son, and nothing more:
Nor to no purpose shalt thou have been given
Into my power. Think not, that I will honour
That ancient love, which so remorselessly
He mangled. They are now past by, those hours

Of friendship and forgiveness. Hate and vengeance
Succeed—'tis now their turn—I too can throw
All feelings of the man aside—can prove
Myself as much a monster as thy father!

   Max. [*calmly.*] Thou wilt proceed with me, as thou hast power.
Thou know'st, I neither brave nor fear thy rage.
What has detained me here, that too thou know'st.
                           [*Taking* THEKLA *by the hand.*
See, Duke! All—all would I have owed to thee,
Would have received from thy paternal hand
The lot of blessed spirits. This hast thou
Laid waste for ever—that concerns not thee.
Indifferent thou tramplest in the dust
Their happiness, who most are thine. The god
Whom thou dost serve, is no benignant deity.
Like as the blind irreconcilable
Fierce element, incapable of compact,
Thy heart's wild impulse only dost thou follow.*

   Wal. Thou art describing thy own father's heart.
The adder! O, the charms of hell o'erpowered me.
He dwelt within me, to my inmost soul
Still to and fro he passed, suspected never!
On the wide ocean, in the starry heaven
Did mine eyes seek the enemy, whom I
In my heart's heart had folded! Had I been

---

* I have here ventured to omit a considerable number of lines, which it is difficult to believe that Schiller could have written.

To *Ferdinand* what Octavio was to *me*,
War had I ne'er denounced against him. No,
I never could have done it. The Emperor was
My austere master only, not my friend.
There was already war 'twixt him and me
When he delivered the Commander's staff
Into my hands; for there's a natural
Unceasing war 'twixt cunning and suspicion;
Peace exists only betwixt confidence
And faith. Who poisons confidence, he murders
The future generations.

 Max.   I will not
Defend my father. Woe is me, I cannot!
Hard deeds and luckless have ta'en place, one
   crime
Drags after it the other in close link.
But we are innocent: how have we fallen
Into this circle of mishap and guilt?
To whom have we been faithless? Wherefore must
The evil deeds and guilt reciprocal
Of our two fathers twine like serpents round us?
        Why must our fathers'
Unconquerable hate rend us asunder,
Who love each other?

 Wal.   Max., remain with me.
Go you not from me, Max.! Hark! I will tell
   thee—
How when at Prague, our winter quarters, thou
Wert brought into my tent a tender boy,
Not yet accustomed to the German winters:

Thy hand was frozen to the heavy colours;
Thou wouldst not let them go.—
At that time did I take thee in my arms,
And with my mantle did I cover thee;
I was thy nurse, no woman could have been
A kinder to thee; I was not ashamed
To do for thee all little offices,
However strange to me; I tended thee
Till life returned; and when thine eyes first
    opened,
I had thee in my arms. Since then, when have I
Altered my feelings t'wards thee? Many thousands
Have I made rich, presented them with lands;
Rewarded them with dignities and honours;
Thee have I *loved:* my heart, my self, I gave
To thee! They were all aliens: THOU wert
Our child and inmate.* Max.! thou canst not
    leave me;
It cannot be; I may not, will not think
That Max. can leave me.
    Max.   O my God!
    Wal.   I have
Held and sustained thee from thy tottering childhood.
What holy bond is there of natural love,

---

* This is a poor and inadequate translation of the affectionate simplicity of the original:—
    Sie alle waren Fremdlinge, *Du* warst
    Das kind des Hauses.
Indeed the whole speech is in the best style of Massinger. O si sic omnia!

What human tie, that does not knit thee to me?
I love thee, Max.! What did thy father for thee,
Which I too have not done, to the height of duty;
Go hence, forsake me, serve thy Emperor;
He will reward thee with a pretty chain
Of gold; with his ram's fleece will he reward
    thee;
For that the friend, the father of thy youth,
For that the holiest feeling of humanity,
Was nothing worth to thee.
  Max.   O God! how can I
Do otherwise? Am I not forced to do it?
My oath—my duty—honour—
  Wal.   How? Thy duty?
Duty to whom? Who art thou? Max.! bethink
    thee
What duties mayst *thou* have? If I am acting
A criminal part toward the Emperor,
It is my crime, not thine. Dost thou belong
To thine own self? Art thou thine own commander?
Stand'st thou, like me, a freeman in the world,
That in thy actions thou shouldst plead free
    agency?
On me thou'rt planted, I am thy Emperor;
To obey *me*, to *belong* to me, this is
Thy honour, this a law of nature to thee!
And if the planet, on the which thou liv'st
And hast thy dwelling, from its orbit starts,
It is not in thy choice, whether or no

Thou'lt follow it;—unfelt it whirls thee onward
Together with his ring and all his moons.
With little guilt stepp'st thou into this contest,
Thee will the world not censure, it will praise thee
For that thou held'st thy friend more worth to thee
Than names and influences more removed.
For justice is the virtue of the ruler,
Affection and fidelity the subject's.
Not every one doth it beseem to question
The far-off high Arcturus.   Most securely
Wilt thou pursue the nearest duty—let
The pilot fix his eye upon the pole-star.

SCENE VII.—*To these enter* NEUMANN.

Wal. What now?
Neu.   The Pappenheimers are dismounted,
And are advancing now on foot, determined
With sword in hand to storm the house, and free
The Count, their colonel.
Wal. [*to* TERTSKY.] Have the cannon planted.
I will receive them with chain-shot. [*Exit* TERTSKY.
Prescribe to me with sword in hand! Go, Neu-
   mann!
'Tis my command that they retreat this moment,
And in their ranks in silence wait my pleasure.
       [NEUMANN *exit.* ILLO *steps to the window.*
Coun. Let him go, I entreat thee, let him go.
Illo. [*at the window.*] Hell and perdition!
Wal.   What is it?

Illo. They scale the council-house, the roof's
    uncovered.
They level at this house the cannon—
   Max.   Madmen!
   Illo. They are making preparations now to fire
    on us.
Duch. and Coun. Merciful Heaven!
   Max. [*to* WALLENSTEIN.] Let me go to them!
   Wal.   Not a step!
   Max. [*pointing to* THEKLA *and the* DUCHESS.]
    But their life! Thine!
Wal.   What tidings bring'st thou, Tertsky?

SCENE VIII.—*To these* TERTSKY (*returning.*)

   Ter. Message and greeting from our faithful
    reg'ments.
Their ardour may no longer be curbed in.
They intreat permission to commence th' attack,
And if thou wouldst but give the word of onset,
They could now charge the enemy in rear,
Into the city wedge them, and with ease
O'erpower them in the narrow streets.
   Illo.   O come!
Let not their ardour cool. The soldiery
Of Butler's corps stand by us faithfully;
We are the greater number. Let us charge
    them,
And finish here in Pilsen the revolt.

Wal. What? shall this town become a field of slaughter,
And brother-killing discord, fire-eyed,
Be let loose through its streets to roam and rage?
Shall the decision be delivered over
To deaf remorseless rage, that hears no leader?
Here is not room for battle, only for butchery.
Well, let it be! I have long thought of it,
So let it burst then! [*Turns to* MAX.
Well, how is it with thee?
Wilt thou attempt a heat with me. Away!
Thou art free to go. Oppose thyself to me.
Front against front, and lead them to the battle;
Thou'rt skilled in war, thou hast learned somewhat under me,
I need not be ashamed of my opponent,
And never hadst thou fairer opportunity
To pay me for thy schooling.
  Coun. Is it then,
Can it have come to this?—What! Cousin! Cousin!
Have you the heart?
  Max. The regiments that are trusted to my care
I have pledged my troth to bring away from Pilsen
True to the Emperor, and this promise will I
Make good, or perish. More than this no duty
Requires of me. I will not fight against thee,
Unless compelled; for though an enemy,
Thy head is holy to me still.
  [*Two reports of cannon.* ILLO *and* TERTSKY *hurry to the window.*

Wal. What's that?
Ter. He falls.
Wal. Falls! Who?
Illo. Tiefenbach's corps.
Discharged the ordnance.
Wal. Upon whom?
Illo. On Neumann,
Your messenger.
Wal. [*starting up.*] Ha! Death and hell! I
  will—
Ter. Expose thyself to their blind frenzy?
Duch. and Coun. No!
For God's sake, no!
Illo. Not yet, my general!
Coun. O, hold him! hold him!
Wal. Leave me——
Max. Do it not;
Not yet! This rash and bloody deed has thrown
  them
Into a frenzy-fit—allow them time——
Wal. Away! too long already have I loitered.
They are emboldened to these outrages,
Beholding not my face. They shall behold
My countenance, shall hear my voice——
Are they not *my* troops? Am I not their General,
And their long-feared commander! Let me see
Whether indeed they do no longer know
That countenance, which was their sun in battle!
From the balcony (mark!) I show myself
To these rebellious forces, and at once

Revolt is mounded, and the high-swoln current
Shrinks back into the old bed of obedience.
    [*Exit* WALLENSTEIN; ILLO, TERTSKY, *and* BUTLER
        follow.

SCENE IX.—COUNTESS, DUCHESS, MAX. *and* THEKLA.

  Coun. [*to the* DUCHESS.] Let them but see
        him—there is hope, still, sister.
Duch. Hope! I have none!
Max. [*who during the last scene has been standing at a distance, in a visible struggle of feelings, advances.*] This can I not endure.
With most determined soul did I come hither,
My purposed action seemed unblamable
To my own conscience—and I must stand here
Like one abhorred, a hard inhuman being;
Yea, loaded with the curse of all I love!
Must see all whom I love in this sore anguish,
Whom I with one word can make happy—O!
My heart revolts within me, and two voices
Make themselves audible within my bosom.
My soul's benighted; I no longer can
Distinguish the right track. O well and truly
Didst thou say, father, I relied too much
On my own heart. My mind moves to and fro—
I know not what to do.
  Coun.   What? you know not?
Does not your own heart tell you? Oh! then I
Will tell it you. Your father is a traitor,

A frightful traitor to us—he has plotted
Against our General's life, has plunged us all
In misery—and you're his son! 'Tis yours
To make the *amends*—Make you the son's fide-
    lity
Outweigh the father's treason, that the name
Of Piccolomini be not a proverb
Of infamy, a common form of cursing
To the posterity of Wallenstein.
  Max. Where is that voice of truth which I dare
    follow?
It speaks no longer in *my* heart. We all
But utter what our passionate wishes dictate:
O that an angel would descend from Heaven,
And scoop for me the right, the uncorrupted,
With a pure hand from the pure fount of Light.
                    [*His eyes glance on* THEKLA.
What other angel seek I? To this heart,
To this unerring heart, will I submit it,
Will ask thy love, which has the power to bless
The happy man alone, averted ever
From the disquieted and guilty—*canst* thou
Still love me if I stay? Say that thou canst,
And I am the Duke's——
  Coun.   Think, niece——
  Max.•   Think nothing, Thekla!
Speak what thou *feelest*.
  Coun.   Think upon your father.
  Max. I did not question thee as Friedland's
    daughter.

Thee, the beloved and unerring god
Within thy heart, I question.   What's at stake?
Not whether diadem of royalty
Be to be won or not—that mightst thou *think* on.
Thy friend, and *his* soul's quiet, are at stake;
The fortune of a thousand gallant men,
Who will all follow me; shall I forswear
My oath and duty to the Emperor?
Say, shall I send into Octavio's camp
The parricidal ball?   For when the ball
Has left its cannon, and is on its flight,
It is no longer a dead instrument!
It lives, a spirit passes into it,
The avenging furies seize possession of it,
And with sure malice guide it the worst way.

   Thek. O! Max.——

   Max. [*interrupting her.*] Nay, not precipitately either, Thekla.
I understand thee.   To thy noble heart,
The hardest duty might appear the highest.
The human, not the great part, would I act.
Ev'n from my childhood to this present hour,
Think what the Duke has done for me, how loved me,
And think too, how my father has repaid him.
O likewise the free lovely impulses
Of hospitality, the pious friend's
Faithful attachment, these too are a holy
Religion to the heart; and heavily
The shudderings of nature do avenge

Themselves on the barbarian that insults them.
Lay all upon the balance, all—then speak,
And let thy heart decide it.
   Thek.   O, thy own
Hath long ago decided. Follow thou
Thy heart's first feeling——
   Coun.   Oh! ill-fated woman!
   Thek. Is it possible that that can be the right,
The which thy tender heart did not at first
Detect and seize with instant impulse? Go,
Fulfil thy duty! I should ever love thee.
Whate'er thou hadst chosen, thou wouldst still have
       acted
Nobly and worthy of thee—but repentance
Shall ne'er disturb thy soul's fair peace.
   Max.   Then I
Must leave thee, must part from thee!
   Thek.   Being faithful
To thine own self, thou art faithful too to me:
If our fates part, our hearts remain united.
A bloody hatred will divide for ever
The houses Piccolomini and Friedland;
But we belong not to our houses—Go!
Quick! quick! and separate thy righteous
       cause
From our unholy and unblessed one!
The curse of Heaven lies upon our head:
'Tis dedicate to ruin. Even me
My father's guilt drags with it to perdition.
Mourn not for me:

My destiny will quickly be decided.

> [MAX. *clasps her in his arms in extreme emotion. There is heard from behind the Scene a loud, wild, long continued cry,* Vivat FERDINANDUS! *accompanied by warlike instruments.* MAX. *and* THEKLA *remain without motion in each other's embraces.*

SCENE X.—*To these enter* TERTSKY.

Coun. [*meeting him.*] What meant that cry? What was it?
Ter.   All is lost!   [tenance?
Coun. What! they regarded not his coun-
Ter. 'Twas all in vain.
Duch. They shouted Vivat!
Ter.   To the Emperor.
Coun. The traitors!
Ter.   Nay! he was not once permitted
Even to address them. Soon as he began,
With deafening noise of warlike instruments
They drowned his words. But here he comes.

SCENE XI.—*To these enter* WALLENSTEIN, *accompanied by* ILLO *and* BUTLER.

Wal. [*as he enters.*] Tertsky!
Ter. My General?
Wal.   Let our regiments hold themselves
In readiness to march; for we shall leave
Pilsen ere evening.   [*Exit* TERTSKY.
            Butler!

THE DEATH OF WALLENSTEIN. 253

But.   Yes, my General.

Wal. The Governor at Egra is your friend
And countryman.   Write to him instantly
By a post-courier.   He must be advised,
That we are with him early on the morrow.
You follow us yourself, your regiment with you.

But. It shall be done, my General!

Wal. [*steps between* MAX. *and* THEKLA, *who
have remained in each other's arms during this
time.*] Part!

Max.   O God!

[Cuirassiers *enter with drawn swords, and assemble in
the back-ground. At the same time there are heard
from below some spirited passages out of the Pappen-
heim March, which seem to address* MAX.

Wal. [*to the* Cuirassiers.] Here he is, he is at
liberty: I keep him
No longer.

[*He turns away, and stands so that* MAX. *cannot pass by
him nor approach the* PRINCESS.

Max. Thou know'st that I have not yet learnt
to live
Without thee!   I go forth into a desert,
Leaving my all behind me.   O do not turn
Thine eyes away from me!   O once more show me
Thy ever dear and honoured countenance.

[MAX. *attempts to take his hand, but is repelled; he
turns to the* COUNTESS.

Is there no eye that has a look of pity for me?

[*The* COUNTESS *turns away from him; he turns to the*
DUCHESS.

My mother!

Duch. Go where duty calls you. Haply
The time may come, when you may prove to us
A true friend, a good angel at the throne
Of the Emperor.

Max. You give me hope; you would not
Suffer me wholly to despair. No! no!
Mine is a certain misery—thanks to Heaven
That offers me a means of ending it.

[*The military music begins again. The Stage fills more and more with armed men.* MAX. *sees* BUTLER, *and addresses him.*

And you here, Colonel Butler—and will you
Not follow me? Well, then! remain more faithful
To your new lord, than you have proved yourself
To the Emperor. Come, Butler! promise me,
Give me your hand upon it, that you'll be
The guardian of his life, its shield, its watchman.
He is attainted, and his princely head
Fair booty for each slave that trades in murder.
Now he doth need the faithful eye of friendship,
And those whom here I see—

[*Casting suspicious looks on* ILLO *and* BUTLER.

Illo. Go—seek for traitors
In Galas', in your father's quarters. Here
Is only one. Away! away! and free us
From his detested sight! Away!

[MAX. *attempts once more to approach* THEKLA. WALLENSTEIN *prevents him.* MAX. *stands irresolute, and in apparent anguish. In the mean time the stage fills more and more; and the horns sound from below louder, and each time after a shorter interval.*

Max. Blow, blow! O were it but the Swedish
    trumpets,
And all the naked swords which I see here,
Were plunged into my breast! What purpose you?
You come to tear me from this place! Beware,
Ye drive me not to desperation.—Do it not!
Ye may repent it!

   [*The stage is entirely filled with armed men.*
Yet more! weight upon weight to drag me down!
Think what ye're doing. It is not well done
To choose a man despairing for your leader;
You tear me from my happiness. Well, then,
I dedicate your souls to vengeance. Mark!
For your own ruin you have chosen me:
Who goes with me must be prepared to perish.

   [*He turns to the back-ground; there ensues a sudden and
   violent movement among the* Cuirassiers; *they sur-
   round him, and carry him off in wild tumult.* WAL-
   LENSTEIN *remains immovable.* THEKLA *sinks
   into her mother's arms. The curtain falls. The
   music becomes loud and overpowering, and passes
   into a complete war march—the orchestra joins it—
   and continues during the interval between the second
   and third Act.*

ACT III.

SCENE I.—*The Burgomaster's House at Egra.*—BUTLER.

But. [*just arrived.*] Here then he is, by his
    destiny conducted.
Here, Friedland! and no farther! From Bohemia
Thy meteor rose, traversed the sky awhile,
And here upon the borders of Bohemia
Must sink.
        Thou hast forsworn the ancient colours.
Blind man! yet trustest to thy ancient fortunes.
Profaner of the altar and the hearth,
Against thy Emperor and fellow-citizens
Thou mean'st to wage the war. Friedland
    beware—
The evil spirit of revenge impels thee—
Beware thou, that revenge destroy thee not!

SCENE II.—BUTLER *and* GORDON.

Gor. Is it you?
How my heart sinks! The Duke a fugitive traitor!
His princely head attainted! O my God!
  But. You have received the letter which I sent
    you

By a post-courier?—

Gor.   Yes! and in obedience to it
Opened the strong hold to him without scruple.
For an imperial letter orders me
To follow your commands implicitly.
But yet forgive me; when even now I saw
The Duke himself, my scruples recommenced.
For truly, not like an attainted man,
Into this town did Friedland make his entrance;
His wonted majesty beamed from his brow,
And calm, as in the days when all was right,
Did he receive from me the accounts of office;
Tis said, that fallen pride learns condescension:
But sparing and with dignity the Duke
Weighed every syllable of approbation,
As masters praise a servant who has done
His duty, and no more.

But.   'Tis all precisely
As I related in my letter. Friedland
Has sold the army to the enemy,
And pledged himself to give up Prague and Egra.
On this report the regiments all forsook him,
The five excepted that belonged to Tertsky,
And which have followed him as thou hast seen.
The sentence of attainder is passed on him,
And every loyal subject is required
To give him into justice, dead or living.

Gor. A traitor to the Emperor—such a noble!
Of such high talents! What is human greatness!
I often said, this can't end happily.

His might, his greatness, and this obscure power,
Are but a covered pit-fall.   The human being
May not be trusted to self-government.
The clear and written law, the deep trod footmarks
Of ancient custom, are all necessary
To keep him in the road of faith and duty.
The authority intrusted to this man
Was unexampled and unnatural;
It placed him on a level with his Emperor,
Till the proud soul unlearned submission.   Woe
   is me;
I mourn for him! for where he fell, I deem
Might none stand firm.   Alas! dear General,
We in our lucky mediocrity
Have ne'er experienced, cannot calculate,
What dangerous wishes such a height may breed
In the heart of such a man.

  But.   Spare your laments
Till he need sympathy; for at this present
He is still mighty, and still formidable.
The Swedes advance to Egra by forced marches,
And quickly will the junction be accomplished.
This must not be!   The Duke must never leave
This strong hold on free footing; for I have
Pledged life and honour here to hold him prisoner,
And your assistance 'tis on which I calculate.

  Gor. O that I had not lived to see this day!
From his hand I received this dignity,
He did himself intrust this strong hold to me,
Which I am now required to make his dungeon.

We subalterns have no will of our own:
The free, the mighty man alone may listen
To the fair impulse of his human nature.
Ah! we are but the poor tools of the law,
Obedience the sole virtue we dare aim at!

But. Nay, let it not afflict you, that your power
Is circumscribed. Much liberty, much error!
The narrow path of duty is securest.

Gor. And all then have deserted him, you say?
He has built up the luck of many thousands;
For kingly was his spirit: his full hand
Was ever open! Many a one from dust
              [*With a side glance on* BUTLER.
Hath he selected, from the very dust
Hath raised him into dignity and honour.
And yet no friend, not one friend hath he purchased,
Whose heart beats true to him in the evil hour.

But. Here's one, I see.

Gor.   I have enjoyed from him
No grace or favour. I could almost doubt,
If ever in his greatness he once thought on
An old friend of his youth. For still my office
Kept me at distance from him; and when first
He to this citadel appointed me,
He was sincere and serious in his duty.
I do not then abuse his confidence,
If I preserve my fealty in that
Which to my fealty was first delivered.

But. Say, then, will you fulfil the attainder on him?

Gor. [*pauses, reflecting, then as in deep dejection.*] If it be so—if all be as you say—
If he've betrayed the Emperor, his master,
Have sold the troops, have purposed to deliver
The strong holds of the country to the enemy—
Yea, truly!—there is no redemption for him!
Yet it is hard, that me the lot should destine
To be the instrument of his perdition;
For we were pages at the court of Bergau
At the same period; but I was the senior.

But. I have heard so——

Gor. 'Tis full thirty years since then
A youth who scarce had seen his twentieth year
Was Wallenstein, when he and I were friends:
Yet even then he had a daring soul:
His frame of mind was serious and severe
Beyond his years: his dreams were of great
objects.
He walked amidst us of a silent spirit,
Communing with himself: yet I have known him
Transported on a sudden into utterance
Of strange conceptions; kindling into splendour
His soul revealed itself, and he spake so
That we looked round perplexed upon each other,
Not knowing whether it were craziness,
Or whether it were a god that spoke in him.

But. But was it where he fell two story high
From a window-ledge, on which he had fallen
asleep;
And rose up free from injury? From this day

(It is reported) he betrayed clear marks
Of a distempered fancy.
 Gor.   He became
Doubtless more self-enwrapt and melancholy;
He made himself a Catholic. Marvellously
His marvellous preservation had transformed him.
Thenceforth he held himself for an exempted
And privileged being, and, as if he were
Incapable of dizziness or fall,
He ran along the unsteady rope of life.
But now our destinies drove us asunder:
He paced with rapid step the way of greatness,
Was Count, and Prince, Duke-regent, and Dic-
  tator.
And now is all, all this too little for him;
He stretches forth his hands for a king's crown,
And plunges in unfathomable ruin.
 But. No more, he comes.

Scene III.—*To these enter* Wallenstein, *in conversation with the* Burgomaster of Egra.

 Wal. You were at one time a free town. I see,
Ye bear the half eagle in your city arms.
Why the *half* eagle only?
 Burg.   We were free,
But for these last two hundred years has Egra
Remained in pledge to the Bohemian crown,
Therefore we bear the half eagle, the other half
Being cancelled till the empire ransom us,

If ever that should be.
 Wal.   Ye merit freedom.
Only be firm and dauntless. Lend your ears
To no designing whispering court-minions.
What may your imposts be?
 Burg.   So heavy that
We totter under them. The garrison
Lives at our costs.
 Wal.   I will relieve you. Tell me,
There are some Protestants among you still?
      [*The* BURGOMASTER *hesitates.*
Yes, yes; I know it. Many lie concealed
Within these walls—Confess now—you yourself—
   [*Fixes his eye on him. The* BURGOMASTER *alarmed.*
Be not alarmed. I hate the Jesuits.
Could my will have determined it, they had
Been long ago expelled the empire. Trust me—
Mass-book or Bible—'tis all one to me.
Of that the world has had sufficient proof.
I built a church for the reformed in Glogan
At my own instance. Hark'e, Burgomaster!
What is your name?
 Burg.   Pachhälbel, may it please you.
 Wal. Hark'e!——
But let it go no further, what I now
Disclose to you in confidence.
   [*Laying his hand on the* BURGOMASTER'S *shoulder, with
    a certain solemnity.*
          The times
Draw near to the fulfilment, Burgomaster!
The high will fall, the low will be exalted.

Hark'e! But keep it to yourself! The end
Approaches of the Spanish double monarchy—
A new arrangement is at hand.   You saw
The three moons that appeared at once in the
    Heaven.
  Burg. With wonder and affright!
  Wal.   Whereof did two
Strangely transform themselves to bloody daggers,
And only one, the middle moon, remained
Steady and clear.
  Burg.   We applied it to the Turks.
  Wal. The Turks! That all?—I tell you, that
    two empires
Will set in blood, in the East and in the West,
And Luth'ranism alone remain.
            [*Observing* GORDON *and* BUTLER.
                I'faith,
'Twas a smart cannonading that we heard
This evening, as we journeyed hitherward;
'Twas on our left hand.   Did you hear it here?
  Gor. Distinctly. The wind brought it from
    the South.
  But. It seemed to come from Weiden or from
    Neustadt.
  Wal. 'Tis likely. That's the route the Swedes
    are taking.
How strong is the garrison?
  Gor.   Not quite two hundred
Competent men, the rest are invalids. [Jochim?
  Wal. Good! And how many in the vale of

Gor. Two hundred arquebussiers have I sent
  thither
To fortify the posts against the Swedes.
 Wal. Good! I commend your foresight. At
  the works too
You have done somewhat?
 Gor.   Two additional batteries
I caused to be run up. They were needless.
The Rhine-grave presses hard upon us, General!
 Wal. You have been watchful in your Em-
  peror's service.
I am content with you, Lieutenant-Colonel.
          [*To* BUTLER.
Release the outposts in the vale of Jochim
With all the stations in the enemy's route.
         [*To* GORDON.
Governor, in your faithful hands I leave
My wife, my daughter, and my sister. I
Shall make no stay here, and wait but the arrival
Of letters, to take leave of you, together
With all the regiments.

 SCENE IV.—*To these enter* COUNT TERTSKY.

 Ter. Joy, General, joy! I bring you welcome
  tidings.
 Wal. And what may they be?
 Ter.   There has been an engagement
At Neustadt; the Swedes gained the victory.
 Wal. From whence did you receive the intel-
  ligence!

Ter. A countryman from Tirschenseil con-
    veyed it.
Soon after sunrise did the fight begin!
A troop of the Imperialists from Fachau
Had forced their way into the Swedish camp;
The cannonade continued full two hours;
There were left dead upon the field a thousand
Imperialists, together with their Colonel;
Further than this he did not know.
    Wal.   How came
Imperial troops at Neustadt? Altringer,
But yesterday, stood sixty miles from there.
Count Galas' force collects at Frauenberg,
And have not the full complement. Is it possible,
That Suys perchance had ventured so far onward?
It cannot be.
    Ter.   We shall soon know the whole,
For here comes Illo, full of haste, and joyous.

SCENE V.—*To these enter* ILLO.

Illo. [*to* WALLENSTEIN.] A courier, Duke!
    he wishes to speak with thee.
Ter. [*eagerly.*] Does he bring confirmation of
    the victory?
Wal. [*at the same time.*] What does he bring?
    Whence comes he?
Illo.   From the Rhine-grave.
And what he brings I can announce to you

Beforehand. Seven leagues distant are the
    Swedes;
At Neustadt did Max. Piccolomini
Throw himself on them with the cavalry;
A murderous fight took place! o'erpowered by
    numbers
The Pappenheimers all, with Max. their leader,
        [WALLENSTEIN *shudders and turns pale.*
Were left dead on the field.
    Wal. [*after a pause, in a low voice.*] Where is
        the messenger? Conduct me to him.

[WALLENSTEIN *is going, when* LADY NEUBRUNN
    rushes into the room. Some Servants *follow her and
    run across the Stage.*

Neu. Help! help!
Illo and Tertsky. [*at the same time.*] What now?
Neu.   The Princess!
Wal. and Ter.   Does she know it?
Neu. [*at the same time with them.*] She is dying!
        [*Hurries off the Stage, when* WALLENSTEIN
            and TERTSKY *follow her.*

SCENE VI.—BUTLER *and* GORDON.

Gor. What's this?
But.   She has lost the man she loved—
Young Piccolomini, who fell in the battle.
Gor. Unfortunate lady!
But.   You have heard what Illo

Reporteth, that the Swedes are conquerors,
And marching hitherward. .

Gor. Too well I heard it.

But. They are twelve regiments strong, and there are five
Close by us to protect the Duke. We have
Only my single regiment; and the garrison
Is not two hundred strong.

Gor. 'Tis even so.

But. It is not possible with such small force
To hold in custody a man like him.

Gor. I grant it.

But. Soon the numbers would disarm us,
And liberate him.

Gor. It were to be feared.

But. [*after a pause.*] Know, I am warranty for the event;
With my head have I pledged myself for his,
Must make my word good, cost it what it will,
And if alive we cannot hold him prisoner,
Why—death makes all things certain!

Gor. Butler! what?
Do I understand you? Gracious God! *You* could—

But. He must not live.

Gor. And *you* can do the deed!

But. Either you or I. This morning was his last.

Gor. You would assassinate him!—

But. 'Tis my purpose.

Gor. Who leans with his whole confidence
    upon you!

But. Such is his evil destiny!

Gor.   Your General!
The sacred person of your General!

But. My General he *has been*.

Gor.   That 'tis only
A "*has been*" washes out no villany.
And without judgment passed?

But.   The execution
Is here instead of judgment.

Gor.   This were murder,
Not justice. The most guilty should be heard.

But. His guilt is clear, the Emperor has passed
    judgment,
And we but execute his will.

Gor.   We should not
Hurry to realize a bloody sentence.
A word may be recalled, a life can never be.

But. Despatch in service pleases sovereigns.

Gor. No honest man's ambitious to press for-
    ward
To the hangman's service.

But.   And no brave man loses
His colour at a daring enterprise.

Gor. A brave man hazards life, but not his
    conscience.

But. What then? Shall he go forth anew to
    kindle
The inextinguishable flame of war?

THE DEATH OF WALLENSTEIN. 269

Gor. Seize him, and hold him prisoner—do not
    kill him!
But. Had not the Emperor's army been de-
    feated,
I might have done so.—But 'tis now past by.
Gor. O, wherefore opened I the stronghold to
    him?
But. His destiny and not the place destroys
    him.
Gor. Upon these ramparts, as beseemed a sol-
    dier,
I had fallen, defending the Emperor's citadel!
But. Yes! and a thousand gallant men have
    perished.
Gor. Doing their duty—that adorns the man!
But murder's a black deed, and nature curses it.
But. [*brings out a paper.*] Here is the mani-
    festo which commands us
To gain possession of his person. See—
It is addressed to you as well as me.
Are you content to take the consequences,
If through our fault he escape to the enemy?
Gor. I?—Gracious God!
But.   Take it on yourself.
Let come of it what may, on you I lay it.
Gor. O God in heaven!
But.   Can you advise aught else
Wherewith to execute the Emperor's purpose?
Say if you can. For I desire his fall,
Not his destruction.

Gor. Merciful heaven! what must be
I see as clear as you. Yet still the heart
Within my bosom beats with other feelings!
　But. Mine is of harder stuff! Necessity
In her rough school hath steeled me. And this Illo
And Tertsky likewise, they must not survive him.
　Gor. I feel no pang for these. Their own bad
　　　hearts
Impelled them, not the influence of the stars.
'Twas they who strewed the seeds of evil passions
In his calm breast, and with officious villany
Watered and nursed the poisonous plants. May
　　　they
Receive their earnests to the uttermost mite!
　But. And their death shall precede his!
We meant to have taken them alive this evening
Amid the merry-making of a feast,
And kept them prisoners in the citadels.
But this makes shorter work. I go this instant
To give the necessary orders.

SCENE VII.—*To these enter* ILLO *and* TERTSKY.

　Ter. Our luck is on the turn. To-morrow come
The Swedes—twelve thousand gallant warriors,
　　　Illo!
Then straightways for Vienna. Cheerily, friend!
What! meet such news with such a moody face?
　Illo. It lies with us at present to prescribe

Laws, and take vengeance on those worthless trai-
    tors,
Those skulking cowards that deserted us;
One has already done his bitter penance,
The Piccolomini, be his the fate
Of all who wish us evil! This flies sure
To the old man's heart; he has his whole life long
Fretted and toiled to raise his ancient house
From a Count's title to the name of Prince;
And now must seek a grave for his only son.

  But. 'Twas pity though! A youth of such heroic
And gentle temp'rament! The Duke himself,
'Twas easily seen, how near it went to his heart,

  Illo. Hark'e, old friend! That is the very point
That never pleased me in our General—
He ever gave the preference to the Italians.
Yea, at this very moment, by my soul
He'd gladly see us all dead ten times over,
Could he thereby recall his friend to life.

  Ter. Hush, hush! Let the dead rest! This
    evening's business
Is, who can fairly drink the other down—
Your regiment Illo! gives the entertainment.
Come! we will keep a merry carnival—
The night for once be day, and mid full glasses
Will we expect the Swedish Avantgarde.

  Illo. Yes, let us be of good cheer for to-day,
For there's hot work before us, friends. This sword
Shall have no rest, till it be bathed to the hilt
In Austrian blood.

Gor. Shame, shame! what talk is this,
My Lord Field Marshal? wherefore foam you so
Against your Emperor?
　　But. 　　Hope not too much
From this first victory. Bethink you, sirs!
How rapidly the wheel of Fortune turns;
The Emperor still is formidably strong.
　　Illo. The Emperor has soldiers, no commander,
For this King Ferdinand of Hungary
Is but a tyro. Galas? He's no luck,
And was of old the ruiner of armies.
And then this viper, this Octavio,
Is excellent at stabbing in the back,
But ne'er meets Friedland in the open field.
　　Ter. Trust me, my friends, it cannot but
　　　　succeed;
Fortune, we know, can ne'er forsake the Duke!
And only under Wallenstein can Austria
Be conqueror.
　　Illo.　　The Duke will soon assemble
A mighty army; all come crowding, streaming
To banners dedicate by destiny
To fame and prosperous fortune. I behold
Old times come back again, he will become
Once more the mighty Lord which he has been.
How will the fools, who've now deserted him,
Look then? I can't but laugh to think of them,
For lands will he present to all his friends,
And like a King and Emperor reward
True services; but we've the nearest claims.

THE DEATH OF WALLENSTEIN.

You will not be forgotten, Governor! [*To* GORDON.
He'll take you from this nest, and bid you shine
In higher station: your fidelity
Well merits it.

Gor.   I am content already,
And wish to climb no higher; where great height is,
The fall must needs be great. "Great height,
    great depth."

Illo. Here you have no more business; for to-
    morrow
The Swedes will take possession of the citadel.
Come, Tertsky, it is supper-time. What think
    you?
Say, shall we have the State illuminated
In honour of the Swede? And who refuses
To do it is a Spaniard and a traitor.

Ter. Nay! Nay! not that, it will not please
    the Duke—

Illo What! we are masters here; no soul shall
    dare
Avow himself imperial where we've rule.
Gordon! Good night, and for the last time,
    take
A fair leave of the place. Send out patrols
To make secure, the watch-word may be altered
At the stroke of ten; deliver in the keys
To the Duke himself, and then you're quit for
    ever
Your wardship of the gates, for on to-morrow
The Swedes will take possession of the citadel.

Ter. [*as he is going, to* BUTLER.] You come
  though to the castle.
But.   At the right time.
    [*Exeunt* TERTSKY *and* ILLO.

SCENE VIII.—GORDON *and* BUTLER.

Gor. [*looking after them.*] Unhappy men!
  How free from all foreboding!
They rush into the outspread net of murder
In the blind drunkenness of victory;
I have no pity for their fate. This Illo,
This overflowing and fool-hardy villain,
That would fain bathe himself in his Emperor's
  blood.
  But. Do as he ordered you. Send round
    patrols,
Take measures for the citadel's security;
When they are within I close the castle gate,
That nothing may transpire.
  Gor. [*with earnest anxiety.*] Oh! haste not so!
Nay, stop; first tell me——
  But.   You have heard already,
To-morrow to the Swedes belongs. This night
Alone is ours. They make good expedition,
But we will make still greater. Fare you well.
  Gor. Ah! your looks tell me nothing good.
    Nay, Butler,
I pray you, promise me!

THE DEATH OF WALLENSTEIN. 275

But.   The sun has set;
A fateful evening doth descend upon us,
And brings on their long night! Their evil stars
Deliver them unarmed into our hands,
And from their drunken dream of golden fortunes
The dagger at their heart shall rouse them. Well
The Duke was ever a great calculator;
His fellow-men were figures on his chess-board,
To move and station as his game required.
Other men's honour, dignity, good name,   [of it:
Did he shift like pawns, and made no conscience
Still calculating, calculating still;
And yet at last his calculation proves
Erroneous; the whole game is lost; and lo!
His own life will be found among the forfeits.

    Gor. O think not of his errors now; remember
His greatness, his munificence, think on all
The lovely features of his character,
On all the noble exploits of his life,
And let them, like an angel's arm, unseen
Arrest the lifted sword.

    But.   It is too late.
I suffer not myself to feel compassion,
Dark thoughts and bloody are my *duty* now:
                        [*Grasping* GORDON's *hand.*
Gordon! 'Tis not my hatred (I pretend not
To love the Duke, and have no cause to love him)
Yet 'tis not now my hatred that impels me
To be his murderer. 'Tis his evil fate.
Hostile concurrences of many events

Control and subjugate me to the office.
In vain the human being meditates
Free action. He is but the wire-worked puppet
Of the blind power, which out of his own choice
Creates for him a dread necessity.
What too would it avail him, if there were
A something pleading for him in my heart—
Still I must kill him.

Gor. If your heart speak to you,
Follow its impulse. 'Tis the voice of God.
Think you your fortunes will grow prosperous
Bedewed with blood—his blood? Believe it not!

But. You know not. Ask not! Wherefore should it happen,
That the Swedes gained the victory, and hasten
With such forced marches hitherward? Fain would I [Gordon!
Have given him to the Emperor's mercy—
I do not wish his blood—But I must ransom
The honour of my word—it lies in pledge—
And he must die, or——

[*Passionately grasping* Gordon's *hand.*

Listen, then, and know!
I am *dishonoured* if the Duke escape us.

Gor. O to save such a man——

But. What!

Gor. It is worth
A sacrifice.—Come, friend! be noble-minded!
Our own heart, and not other men's opinions,
Forms our true honour.

But. [*with a cold and haughty air.*] He is a
    great Lord,
This Duke—and I am but of mean importance!
This is what you would say. Wherein concerns it
The world at large, you mean to hint to me,
Whether the man of low extraction keeps
Or blemishes his honour—
So that the man of princely rank be saved.
We all do stamp our value on ourselves.
The price we challenge for ourselves is given us.
There does not live on earth the man so stationed,
That I despise myself compared with him.
Man is made great or little by his own will:
Because I am true to mine, therefore he dies.

   Gor. I am endeavouring to move a rock.
Thou hadst a mother, yet no human feelings.
I cannot hinder you, but may some god
Rescue him from you!   [*Exit* GORDON.

    SCENE IX.—BUTLER *alone.*

I treasured my good name all my life long;
The Duke has cheated me of life's best jewel,
So that I blush before this poor weak Gordon!
He prizes above all his fealty;
His conscious soul accuses him of nothing;
In opposition to his own soft heart
He subjugates himself to an iron duty.
Me in a weaker moment passion warped;
I stand beside him, and must feel myself

The worst man of the two. What, though the world
Is ignorant of my purposed treason, yet
One Man does know it, and can prove it too—
High-minded Piccolomini!
There lives the man who can dishonour me!
This ignominy blood alone can cleanse!
Duke Friedland, thou or I—Into my own hands
Fortune delivers me—The dearest thing a man has is himself.

The Curtain drops.

ACT IV.

Scene I.—Butler's *Chamber.*

Butler, *and* Major Geraldin.

But. Find me twelve strong dragoons, arm them with pikes,
For there must be no firing;——
Conceal them somewhere near the banquet-room,
And soon as the dessert is served up, rush all in
And cry,—Who is loyal to the Emperor?
I will overturn the table—while you attack
Illo and Tertsky, and dispatch them both.

The castle-palace is well barred and guarded,
That no intelligence of this proceeding
May make its way to the Duke.—Go instantly;
Have you yet sent for Captain Devereux
And the Macdonald?———

Ger.   They'll be here anon.
                        [*Exit* GERALDIN.

But. Here's no room for delay. The citizens
Declare for him, a dizzy drunken spirit
Possesses the whole town. They see in the Duke
A Prince of peace, a founder of new ages
And golden times. Arms too have been given out
By the town-council, and a hundred citizens
Have volunteered themselves to stand on guard.
Despatch then be the word. For enemies
Threaten us from without and from within.

    SCENE II.—BUTLER, CAPTAIN DEVEREUX *and*
                MACDONALD.

Mac. Here we are, General.
Dev.   What's to be the watchword?
But. Long live the Emperor!
Both. [*recoiling.*] How?
But.   Live the house of Austria!
Dev. Have we not sworn fidelity to Friedland?
Mac. Have we not marched to this place to
      protect him?
But. Protect a traitor, and his country's enemy!

Dev. Why, yes! in his name you administered
Our oath.

Mac. And followed him yourself to Egra.

But. I did it the more surely to destroy him.

Dev. So then!

Mac.   An altered case!

But. [*to* DEVEREUX.]   Thou wretched man!
So easily leav'st thou thy oath and colours?

Dev. The devil!—I but followed your example,
If you could prove a villain, why not we?

Mac. We've nought to do with *thinking*—that's
      your business.
You are our General, and give out the orders!
We follow you, though the track lead to hell.

But. [*appeased.*] Good, then! we know each
      other.

Mac.   I should hope so.

Dev. Soldiers of fortune are we—who bids most,
He has us.

Mac. 'Tis e'en so!

But.   Well, for the present
Ye must remain honest and faithful soldiers:——

Dev. We wish no other.

But.   Ay, and make your fortunes.

Mac. That is still better.

But.   Listen!

Both.   We attend.

But. It is the Emperor's will and ordinance
To seize the person of the Prince-Duke Friedland,
Alive or dead.

Dev. It runs so in the letter.
Mac. Alive or dead—these were the very words.
But. And he shall be rewarded from the State
In land and gold, who proffers aid thereto.
Dev. Ay? That sounds well. The *words* sound always well,
That travel hither from the Court. Yes! yes!
We know already what Court-words import.
A golden chain perhaps in sign of favour,
Or an old charger, or a parchment patent,
And such like.—The Prince-Duke pays better.
Mac. Yes,
The Duke's a splendid paymaster.
But. All over
With that, my friends! His lucky stars are set.
Mac. And is that certain?
But. You have my word for it.
Dev. His lucky fortunes all past by?
But. For ever.
He is as poor as we.
Mac. As poor as we?
Dev. Macdonald, we'll desert him.
But. We'll desert him!
Full twenty thousand have done that already;
We must do more, my countrymen! In short—
We—we must kill him.
Both. [*starting back.*] Kill him!
But. Yes! must kill him!
And for that purpose have I chosen you.
Both. Us!

But. You, Captain Devereux, and thee, Macdonald.

Dev. [*after a pause.*] Choose you some other.

But. What? art dastardly?
Thou, with full thirty lives to answer for—
Thou conscientious of a sudden?

Dev. Nay,
To assassinate our Lord and General—

Mac. To whom we've sworn a soldier's oath—

But. The oath
Is null, for Friedland is a traitor.

Dev. No, no! It is too bad!

Mac. Yes, by my soul!
It is too bad. One has a conscience too—

Dev. If it were not our chieftain, who so long
Has issued the commands, and claim'd our duty,——

But. Is that the objection?

Dev. Were it my own father,
And the Emperor's service should demand it of me,
It might be done perhaps—But we are soldiers,
And to assassinate our chief commander,
That is a sin, a foul abomination,
From which no monk or confessor absolves us.

But. I am your Pope, and give you absolution.
Determine quickly!

Dev. 'Twill not do!

Mac. 'Twon't do.

But. Well, off, then! and—send Pestalutz to me.

Dev. [*hesitates.*] The Pestalutz—
Mac. What may you want with him?
But. If you reject it, we can find enough—
Dev. Nay, if he must fall, we may earn the bounty
As well as any other. What think you,
Brother Macdonald?
Mac. Why if he *must* fall,
And *will* fall, and it can't be otherwise,
One would not give place to this Pestalutz.
Dev. [*after some reflection.*] When do you purpose he should fall?
But. This night;—
To-morrow will the Swedes be at our gates.
Dev. You take upon you all the consequences!
But. I take the whole upon me.
Dev. And it is
The Emperor's will, his express absolute will?—
For we have instances, that folks may like
The murder, and yet hang the murderer.
But. The manifesto says—alive or dead.
Alive—it is not possible—you see it is not.
Dev. Well, dead then! dead! But how can we come at him?
The town is fill'd with Tertsky's soldiery.
Mac. Ay! and then Tertsky still remains, and Illo—
But. With these you shall begin—you understand me?
Dev. How? And must they too perish?

But.   They the first.
Mac. Hear, Devereux! A bloody evening this.
Dev. Have you a man for that? Commission
           me—
But. 'Tis given in trust to Major Geraldin;
This is a carnival night, and there's a feast
Given at the castle—there we shall surprise them,
And hew them down. The Pestalutz, and Lesley
Have that commission—soon as that is finished—
  Dev. Hear, General! It will be all one to you.
Hark'e! let me exchange with Geraldin.
  But. 'Twill be the lesser danger with the Duke.
  Dev. Danger! The Devil! What do you think
           me, General?
'Tis the Duke's eye, and not his sword, I fear.
  But. What can his eye do to thee?
  Dev.   Death and hell!
Thou know'st that I'm no milk-sop, General!
But 'tis not eight days since the Duke did send me
Twenty gold pieces for this good warm coat
Which I have on! and then for him to see me
Standing before him with the pike, his murderer,
That eye of his looking upon this coat—
Why—why—the devil fetch me! I'm no milk-sop!
  But. The Duke presented thee this good warm
           coat,
And thou, a needy wight, has pangs of conscience
To run him through the body in return.
A coat that is far better and far warmer
Did the Emperor give to him, the Prince's mantle.

How doth he thank the Emperor? With revolt
And treason!

Dev. That is true. The devil take
Such thankers! I'll dispatch him.

But. And would'st quiet
Thy conscience, thou hast nought to do but simply
Pull off the coat; so canst thou do the deed
With light heart and good spirits.

Dev. You are right.
That did not strike me. I'll pull off the coat—
So there's an end of it.

Mac. Yes, but there's another
Point to be thought of.

But. And what's that, Macdonald?

Mac. What avails sword or dagger against *him*?
He is not to be wounded—he is—

But. [*starting up.*] What?

Mac. Safe against shot, and stab and flash!
      Hard frozen,
Secured, and warranted by the black art!
His body is impenetrable, I tell you.

Dev. In Inglestadt there was just such another;
His whole skin was the same as steel; at last
We were obliged to beat him down with gun-
      stocks.

Mac. Hear what I'll do.

Dev. Well?

Mac. In the cloister here
There's a Dominican, my countryman.
I'll make him dip my sword and pike for me

In holy water, and say over them
One of his strongest blessings. That's probatum!
Nothing can stand 'gainst that.
  But. So do, Macdonald!
But now go and select from out the regiment
Twenty or thirty able-bodied fellows,
And let them take the oaths to the Emperor.
Then when it strikes eleven, when the first rounds
Are passed, conduct them silently as may be
To th' house—I will myself be not far off.
  Dev. But how do we get through Hartschier
      and Gordon,
That stand on guard there in the inner chamber?
  But. I have made myself acquainted with the
      place.
I lead you through a back door that's defended
By one man only. Me my rank and office
Give access to the Duke at every hour.
I'll go before you—with one poniard-stroke
Cut Hartschier's wind-pipe, and make way for you.
  Dev. And when we are there, by what means
      shall we gain
The Duke's bed-chamber, without his alarming
The servants of the Court; for he has here
A numerous company of followers?
  But. The attendants fill the right wing; he
      hates bustle,
And lodges in the left wing quite alone.
  Dev. Were it well over—hey, Macdonald? I
Feel queerly on the occasion, devil knows!

Mac. And I too. 'Tis too great a personage.
People will hold us for a brace of villains.
    But. In plenty, honour, splendour—You may safely
Laugh at the people's babble.
    Dev.   If the business
Squares with one's honour—if that be quite certain—
    But. Set your hearts quite at ease. Ye save for Ferdinand
His Crown and Empire. The reward can be
No small one.
    Dev. And 'tis his purpose to dethrone the Emperor?
    But. Yes!—Yes!—to rob him of his crown and life.
    Dev. And he must fall by the executioner's hands,
Should we deliver him up to the Emperor
Alive?
    But. It were his certain destiny.
    Dev. Well! Well! Come then, Macdonald, he shall not
Lie long in pain.
    [*Exeunt* BUTLER *through one door*, MACDONALD *and* DEVEREUX *through the other.*

SCENE III.—*A Gothic and gloomy Apartment at the* DUCHESS FRIEDLAND'S. THEKLA *on a seat, pale, her eyes closed. The* DUCHESS *and* LADY NEUBRUNN *busied about her.* WALLENSTEIN *and the* COUNTESS *in conversation ?*

Wal. How knew she it so soon?
Coun.   She seems to have
Foreboded some misfortune. The report
Of an engagement, in the which had fallen
A colonel of the imperial army, frightened her.
I saw it instantly. She flew to meet
The Swedish courier, and with sudden questioning,
Soon wrested from him the disastrous secret.
Too late we missed her, hastened after her,
We found her lying in his arms, all pale
And in a swoon.
 Wal.   A heavy, heavy blow!
And she so unprepared! Poor child! How is it?
       [*Turning to the* DUCHESS.
Is she coming to herself?
 Duch.   Her eyes are opening.
 Coun. She lives.
 Thek. [*looking around her.*] Where am I?
 Wal. [*steps to her, raising her up in his arms.*]
Come, cheerly, Thekla! be my own brave girl!
See, there's thy loving mother. Thou art in
Thy father's arms.
 Thek. [*standing up.*] Where is he? Is he gone?
 Duch. Who gone, my daughter?

Thek. He—the man who uttered
That word of misery.

Duch. O! think not of it,
My Thekla!

Wal. Give her sorrow leave to talk!
Let her complain—mingle your tears with hers,
For she hath suffered a deep anguish; but
She'll rise superior to it, for my Thekla
Hath all her father's unsubdued heart.

Thek. I am not ill. See, I have power to stand.
Why does my mother weep? Have I alarmed her?
It is gone by—I recollect myself—

[*She casts her eyes round the room, as seeking some one.*

Where is he? Please you, do not hide him from me,
You see I have strength enough: now I will hear him.

Duch. No, never shall this messenger of evil
Enter again into thy presence, Thekla!

Thek. My father—

Wal. Dearest daughter!

Thek. I'm not weak—
Shortly I shall be quite myself again.
You'll grant me one request?

Wal. Name it, my daughter.

Thek. Permit the stranger to be called to me,
And grant me leave, that by myself I may
Hear his report and question him.

Duch. No, never!

Coun. 'Tis not advisable—assent not to it.

Wal. Hush! Wherefore would'st thou speak
    with him, my daughter?
Thek. Knowing the whole I shall be more col-
    lected;
I will not be deceived. My mother wishes
Only to spare me. I will not be spared.
The worst is said already; I can hear
Nothing of deeper anguish!
    Coun. and Duch.   Do it not.
    Thek. The horror overpowered me by surprise.
My heart betrayed me in the stranger's presence;
He was a witness of my weakness, yea,
I sank into his arms; and that has shamed me.
I must replace myself in his esteem,
And I must speak with him, perforce, that he,
The stranger, may not think ungently of me.
    Wal. I see she is in the right, and am inclined
To grant her this request of hers. Go, call him.
        [LADY NEUBRUNN *goes to call him.*
    Duch. But I, thy mother, will be present—
    Thek.   'Twere
More pleasing to me, if alone I saw him:
Trust me, I shall behave myself the more
Collectedly.
    Wal.   Permit her her own will.
Leave her alone with him: for there are sorrows,
Where of necessity the soul must be
Its own support. A strong heart will rely
On its own strength alone. In her own bosom,
Not in her mother's arms, must she collect

The strength to rise superior to this blow.
It is mine own brave girl. I'll have her treated
Not as the woman, but the heroine   [*Going.*
  Coun. [*detaining him.*] Where art thou going?
     I heard Tertsky say
That 'tis *thy* purpose to depart from hence
To-morrow early, but to leave us here.
  Wal. Yes, ye stay here, placed under the protection
Of gallant men.
  Coun.   O take us with you, brother.
Leave us not in this gloomy solitude
To brood o'er anxious thoughts. The mists of doubt
Magnify evils to a shape of horror.
  Wal. Who speaks of evil! I entreat you, sister,
Use words of better omen.
  Coun.   Then take us with you.
O leave us not behind you in a place
That forces us to such sad omens. Heavy
And sick within me is my heart———
These walls breathe on me, like a church-yard vault.
I cannot tell you, brother, how this place
Doth go against my nature. Take us with you.
Come, sister, join you your entreaty!—Niece,
Yours too. We all entreat you, take us with you.
  Wal. The place's evil omens will I change,
Making it that which shields and shelters for me
My best beloved.

Lady Neu. [*returning.*] The Swedish officer.
Wal. Leave her alone with him. [*Exit.*
Duch. [*to* THEKLA, *who starts and shivers.*]
 There—pale as death! Child, 'tis impossible
That thou shouldst speak with him. Follow thy mother.
Thek. The Lady Neubrunn then may stay with me. [*Exeunt* DUCHESS *and* COUNTESS.

SCENE IV.—THEKLA, *the* Swedish Captain, LADY NEUBRUNN.

Cap. [*respectfully approaching her.*] Princess—I must entreat your gentle pardon—
My inconsiderate rash speech—How could I—
 Thek. [*with dignity.*] You did behold me in my agony.
A most distressful accident occasioned
You, from a stranger, to become at once
My confidant.
 Cap. I fear you hate my presence,
For my tongue spake a melancholy word.
 Thek. The fault is mine. Myself did wrest it from you.
The horror which came o'er me interrupted
Your tale at its commencement. May it please you,
Continue it to the end.

Cap.   Princess, 'twill
Renew your anguish.
   Thek.   I am firm.——
I *will* be firm. Well—how began the engage-
        ment?
   Cap. We lay, expecting no attack, at Neustadt,
Entrenched but insecurely in our camp,
When towards evening rose a cloud of dust
From the wood thitherward; our vanguard fled
Into the camp, and sounded the alarm.
Scarce had we mounted, ere the Pappenheimers,
Their horses at full speed, broke through the lines,
And leaped the trenches! but their heedless cou-
        rage
Had borne them onward far before the others—
The infantry were still at distance, only
The Pappenheimers followed daringly
Their daring leader.

   [THEKLA *betrays agitation in her gestures. The* Officer
    pauses till she makes a sign to him to proceed.

             Both in van and flanks
With our whole cavalry we now received them;
Back to the trenches drove them, where the foot
Stretched out a solid ridge of pikes to meet them.
They neither could advance, nor yet retreat;
And as they stood on every side wedged in,
The Rhinegrave to their leader called aloud,
Inviting a surrender; but their leader,
Young Piccolomini——

        [THEKLA, *as giddy, grasps a chair.*

Known by his plume,
And his long hair, gave signal for the trenches;
Himself leaped first, the regiment all plunged after,
His charger, by a halbert gored, reared up,
Flung him with violence off, and over him
The horses, now no longer to be curbed,——

[THEKLA, *who has accompanied the last speech with all the marks of increasing agony, trembles through her whole frame, and is falling. The* LADY NEU-BRUNN *runs to her, and receives her in her arms.*

Neu. My dearest lady——
Cap.   I retire.
Thek.   'Tis over.
Proceed to the conclusion.
Cap.   While despair
Inspired the troops with frenzy when they saw
Their leader perish; every thought of rescue
Was spurned; they fought like wounded tigers;
            their
Frantic resistance roused our soldiery;
A murderous fight took place, nor was the contest
Finished before their last man fell.
    Thek. [*faltering.*]   And where——
Where is—You have not told me all.
    Cap. [*after a pause.*]   This morning
We buried him. Twelve youths of noblest birth
Did bear him to interment; the whole army
Followed the bier. A laurel decked his coffin;
The sword of the deceased was placed upon it,
In mark of honour, by the Rhinegrave's self.

Nor tears were wanting; for there are among us
Many who had themselves experienced
The greatness of his mind, and gentle manners;
All were affected at his fate. The Rhinegrave
Would willingly have saved him; but himself
Made vain the attempt—'tis said he wished to die.
 Neu. [*to* THEKLA, *who has hidden her countenance.*] Look up, my dearest lady——
 Thek.   Where is his grave?
 Cap. At Neustadt, lady; in a cloister church
Are his remains deposited, until
We can receive directions from his father.
 Thek. What is the cloister's name?
 Cap.   Saint Catharine's.
 Thek. And how far is it thither?
 Cap.   Near twelve leagues.
 Thek. And which the way?
 Cap.   You go by Tirschenreit
And Falkenberg through our advanced posts.
 Thek.   Who
Is their commander?
 Cap.   Colonel Seckendorf.
[THEKLA *steps to the table, and takes a ring from a casket.*
 Thek. You have beheld me in my agony,
And shown a feeling heart. Please you, accept
      [*Giving him the ring.*
A small memorial of this hour. Now go!
 Cap. Princess——
  [THEKLA *silently makes signs to him to go, and turns from him. The* Captain *lingers, and is about to speak.* LADY NEUBRUNN *repeats the signal, and he retires.*

SCENE V.—THEKLA, LADY NEUBRUNN.

Thek. [*falls on* LADY NEUBRUNN'S *neck.*] Now,
  gentle Neubrunn, show me the affection
Which thou hast ever promised—prove thyself
My own true friend and faithful fellow-pilgrim.
This night we must away!
 Neu.   Away! and whither?
 Thek. Whither! There is but one place in
  the world.
Thither where he lies buried! To his coffin!
 Neu. What would you do there?
 Thek.   What do there?
That would'st thou not have asked, hadst thou
  e'er loved.
There, there is all that still remains of him.
That single spot is the whole earth to me.
 Neu. That place of death——
 Thek.   Is now the only place,
Where life yet dwells for me: detain me not!
Come and make preparations: let us think
Of means to fly from hence.
 Neu.   Your father's rage——
 Thek. That time is past——
And now I fear no human being's rage.
 Neu. The sentence of the world! the tongue
  of calumny!
 Thek. Whom am I seeking? Him who is no
  more.

Am I then hastening to the arms——O God!
I haste but to the grave of the beloved.
 Neu. And we alone, two helpless feeble women?
 Thek. We will take weapons: my arms shall
   protect thee.
 Neu. In the dark night-time.
 Thek.   Darkness will conceal us.
 Neu. This rough tempestuous night——
 Thek.   Had he a soft bed
Under the hoofs of his war-horses?
 Neu.   Heaven!
And then the many posts of the enemy!—
 Thek. They are human beings. Misery travels
   free
Through the whole earth.
 Neu.   The journey's weary length—
 Thek. The pilgrim travelling to a distant shrine
Of hope and healing, doth not count the leagues.
 Neu. How can we pass the gates?
 Thek.   Gold opens them.
Go, do but go.
 Neu. Should we be recognized—
 Thek. In a despairing woman, a poor fugitive,
Will no one seek the daughter of Duke Friedland.
 Neu. And where procure we horses for our
   flight?
 Thek. My equerry procures them. Go and
   fetch him.
 Neu. Dares he, without the knowledge of his
   lord?

Thek. He will. Go, only go. Delay no longer.
Neu. Dear lady! and your mother?
Thek.   Oh! my mother!
Neu. So much as she has suffered too already;
Your tender mother—Ah! how ill prepared
For this last anguish!
   Thek.   Woe is me! my mother!
                                         [*Pauses.*
Go instantly.
   Neu.   But think what you are doing!
   Thek. What *can* be thought, already has been
        thought.
   Neu. And being there, what purpose you to do?
   Thek. There a divinity will prompt my soul.
   Neu. Your heart, dear lady, is disquieted!
And this is not the way that leads to quiet.
   Thek. To a deep quiet, such as he has found.
It draws me on, I know not what to name it,
Resistless does it draw me to his grave.
There will my heart be eased, my tears will flow,
O hasten, make no further questioning!
There is no rest for me till I have left
These walls—they fall in on me—A dim power
Drives me from hence—Oh mercy! What a
        feeling!
What pale and hollow forms are those! They fill,
They crowd the place! I have no longer room
        here!
Mercy! Still more! More still! The hideous
        swarm!

They press on me; they chase me from these
          walls—
Those hollow, bodiless forms of living men!
  Neu. You frighten me so, lady, that no longer
I dare stay here myself.   I go and call
Rosenberg instantly.   [*Exit* LADY NEUBRUNN.

                SCENE VI.

  Thek. His spirit 'tis that calls me : 'tis the troop
Of his true followers, who offered up
Themselves t'avenge his death: and they accuse
          me
Of an ignoble loitering—*they* would not
Forsake their leader even in his death—*they* died
          for him!
And shall *I* live?——
For me too was that laurel-garland twined
That decks his bier.   Life is an empty casket:
I throw it from me.   O! my only hope ;—
To die beneath the hoofs of trampling steeds—
That is the lot of heroes upon earth!
                            [*Exit* THEKLA.
       The Curtain drops.

ACT V.

SCENE I.—*A Saloon, terminated by a gallery which extends far into the back-ground.* WALLENSTEIN *sitting at a table.* The Swedish Captain *standing before him.*

Wal. Commend me to your lord. I sympathize
In his good fortune; and if you have seen me
Deficient in the expressions of that joy,
Which such a victory might well demand,
Attribute it to no lack of good will,
For henceforth are our fortunes one.   Farewell,
And for your trouble take my thanks.   To-morrow
The citadel shall be surrendered to you
On your arrival.

> [*The* Swedish Captain *retires.* WALLENSTEIN *sits lost in thought, his eyes fixed vacantly, and his head sustained by his hand. The* COUNTESS TERTSKY *enters, stands before him awhile, unobserved by him; at length he starts, sees her, and recollects himself.*

Wal. Com'st thou from her?   Is she restored?
   How is she?
Coun. My sister tells me, she was more collected
After her conversation with the Swede.
She has now retired to rest.
Wal.   The pang will soften,
She will shed tears.

Coun.   I find thee altered too,
My brother! After such a victory
I had expected to have found in thee
A cheerful spirit. O remain *thou* firm!
Sustain, uphold us! For our light thou art,
Our sun.

Wal. Be quiet. I ail nothing. Where's
Thy husband?

Coun.   At a banquet—he and Illo.

Wal. [*rises, and strides across the room.*] The
    night's far spent. Betake thee to thy
    chamber.

Coun. Bid me not go, O let me stay with thee!

Wal. [*moves to the window.*] There is a busy
    motion in the heaven,
The wind doth chase the flag upon the tower,
Fast sweep the clouds, the sickle * of the moon,
Struggling, darts snatches of uncertain light.

---

* These four lines are expressed in the original with exquisite felicity,

    Am Himmel ist geschäftige Bewegung,
    Des Thurmes Fahne jagt der Wind, schnell geht
    Der Wolken Zug, *die Mondes-sichel wankt,*
    Und durch die Nacht zucht ungewisse Helle.

The word "moon-sickle" reminds me of a passage in Harris, as quoted by Johnson, under the word "falcated." "The enlightened part of the moon appears in the form of a sickle or reaping-hook, which is while she is moving from the conjunction to the opposition, or from the new moon to the full; but from full to a new again, the enlightened part appears gibbous, and the dark *falcated.*"

The words "wanken" and "schweben" are not easily translated. The English words, by which we attempt to

No form of star is visible! That one
White stain of light, that single glimmering yonder,
Is from Cassiopeia, and therein
Is Jupiter. [*A pause.*] But now
The blackness of the troubled element hides him!
[*He sinks into profound melancholy, and looks vacantly into the distance.*

Coun. [*looks on him mournfully, then grasps his hand.*] What art thou brooding on?

Wal.   Methinks,
If but I saw him, 'twould be well with me.
He is the star of my nativity,
And often marvellously hath his aspect
Shot strength into my heart.

Coun.   Thou'lt see him again.

Wal. [*remains for a while with absent mind, then assumes a livelier manner, and turns suddenly to the* COUNTESS.] See him again? O never,
     never again.

Coun. How?

Wal.   He is gone—is dust.

Coun.   Whom meanest thou then?

Wal. He, the more fortunate! yea, he hath
     finished!
For him there is no longer any future,
His life is bright—bright without spot it *was*
And cannot cease to be. No ominous hour

---

render them, are either vulgar or pedantic, or not of sufficiently general application. So " der Wolken Zug "—the draft, the procession of clouds.—The masses of the clouds sweep onward in swift *stream*.

Knocks at his door with tidings of mishap.
Far off is he, above desire and fear;
No more submitted to the change and chance
Of the unsteady planets. O 'tis well
With *him!* but who knows what the coming hour
Veil'd in thick darkness brings for us!
 Coun.   Thou speak'st
Of Piccolomini. What was his death?
The courier had just left thee as I came.

 [WALLENSTEIN *by a motion of his hand makes signs to her to be silent.*

Turn not thine eyes upon the backward view,
Let us look forward into sunny days,
Welcome with joyous heart the victory,
Forget what it has cost thee. Not to-day,
For the first time, thy friend was to thee dead;
To thee he died, when first he parted from thee.
 Wal. I shall grieve down this blow, of that I'm
   conscious:
What does not man grieve down? From the
   highest,
As from the vilest thing of every day
He learns to wean himself; for the strong hours
Conquer him. Yet I feel what I have lost
In him. The bloom is vanished from my life.
For O! he stood beside me, like my youth,
Transformed for me the real to a dream,
Clothing the palpable and familiar
With golden exhalations of the dawn.
Whatever fortunes wait my future toils,

The *beautiful* is vanished—and returns not.
  Coun. O be not treacherous to thy own power.
Thy heart is rich enough to vivify
Itself. Thou lov'st and prizest virtues in him,
The which thyself didst plant, thyself unfold.
  Wal. [*stepping to the door.*] Who interrupts us
      now at this late hour?
It is the Governor. He brings the keys
Of the Citadel. 'Tis midnight. Leave me, sister!
  Coun. O 'tis so hard to me this night to leave
      thee—
A boding fear possesses me!
  Wal.   Fear! Wherefore?
  Coun. Should'st thou depart this night, and we
      at waking
Never more find thee!
  Wal.   Fancies!
  Coun.   O my soul
Has long been weighed down by these dark fore-
      bodings.
And if I combat and repel them waking,
They still rush down upon my heart in dreams.
I saw thee yesternight with thy first wife
Sit at a banquet gorgeously attired.
  Wal. This was a dream of favourable omen,
That marriage being the founder of my fortunes.
  Coun. To-day I dreamed that I was seeking
      thee
In thy own chamber. As I entered, lo!
It was no more a chamber;—the Chartreuse

At Gitschin 'twas, which thou thyself hast founded,
And where it is thy will that thou shouldst be
Interred.
    Wal. Thy soul is busy with these thoughts.
    Coun. What dost thou not believe that oft in
        dreams
A voice of warning speaks prophetic to us?
    Wal. There is no doubt that there exists such
        voices.
Yet I would not call *them*
Voices of warning that announce to us
Only the inevitable. As the sun,
Ere it is risen, sometimes paints its image
In the atmosphere, so often do the spirits
Of great events stride on before the events,
And in to-day already walks to-morrow.
That which we read of the fourth Henry's death
Did ever vex and haunt me like a tale
Of my own future destiny. The king
Felt in his breast the phantom of the knife,
Long ere Ravaillac armed himself therewith.
His quiet mind forsook him: the phantasma
Started him in his Louvre, chased him forth
Into the open air: like funeral knells
Sounded that coronation festival:
And still with boding sense he heard the tread
Of those feet that even then were seeking him
Throughout the streets of Paris,
  Coun.   And to *thee*
The voice within thy soul bodes nothing?

Wal.   Nothing.
Be wholly tranquil.
    Coun.   And another time
I hastened after thee, and thou ran'st from me
Through a long suite, through many a spacious hall,
There seemed no end of it: doors creaked and clapped:
I followed panting, but could not o'ertake thee;
When on a sudden did I feel myself
Grasped from behind—the hand was cold that grasped me—
'Twas thou, and thou didst kiss me, and there seemed
A crimson covering to envelope us.
    Wal. That is the crimson tapestry of my chamber.
    Coun. [*gazing on him.*] If it should come to that—if I should see thee,
Who standest now before me in the fulness
Of life—   [*She falls on his breast and weeps.*
    Wal. The Emperor's proclamation weighs upon thee—
Alphabets wound not—and he finds no hands.
    Coun. If he *should* find them, my resolve is taken—
I bear about me my support and refuge.
                               [*Exit* COUNTESS.

Scene II.—Wallenstein, Gordon.

Wal. All quiet in the town?
Gor.   The town is quiet.
Wal. I hear a boisterous music! and the Castle
Is lighted up.   Who are the revellers?
Gor. There is a banquet given at the Castle
To the Count Tertsky, and Field Marshal Illo.
Wal. In honor of the victory.—This tribe
Can show their joy in nothing else but feasting.
          [*Rings. The* Groom of the Chamber *enters.*
Unrobe me, I will lay me down to sleep.
          [Wallenstein *takes the keys from* Gordon.
So we are guarded from all enemies,
And shut in with sure friends.
For all must cheat me, or a face like this
                    [*Fixing his eye on* Gordon.
Was ne'er a hypocrite's mask.
     [*The* Groom of the Chamber *takes off his mantle, collar, and scarf.*
Wal.   Take care—what is that?
Groom of the Chamber. The golden chain is
     snapped in two.
Wal. Well, it has lasted long enough.   Here—
     give it.   [*He takes and looks at the chain.*
'Twas the first present of the Emperor.
He hung it round me in the war of Friule,
He being then Archduke; and I have worn it
Till now from habit——
From superstition if you will.   Belike,

It was to be a talisman to me,
And while I wore it on my neck in faith,
It was to chain to me all my life long,
The volatile fortune, whose first pledge it was.
Well, be it so! Henceforward a new fortune
Must spring up for me! for the potency
Of this charm is dissolved.

> [Groom of the Chamber *retires with the vestments.* WALLENSTEIN *rises, takes a stride across the Room, and stands at last before* GORDON *in a posture of meditation.*

How the old time returns upon me! I
Behold myself once more at Burgau, where
We two were pages of the Court together.
We oftentimes disputed: thy intention
Was ever good; but thou wert wont to play
The moralist and preacher, and would'st rail at
    me—
That I strove after things too high for me,
Giving my faith to bold unlawful dreams,
And still extol to me the golden mean.
—Thy wisdom hath been proved a thriftless friend
To thy own self. See, it has made thee early
A superannuated man, and (but
That my munificent stars will intervene)
Would let thee in some miserable corner
Go out like an untended lamp.

  Gor.   My Prince!
With light heart the poor fisher moors his boat,
And watches from the shore the lofty ship

Stranded amid the storm.
 Wal.   Art thou already
In harbour then, old man? Well! I am not.
The unconquered spirit drives me o'er life's bil-
   lows;
My planks still firm, my canvas swelling proudly,
Hope is my goddess still, and youth my inmate;
And while we stand thus front to front, almost
I might presume to say, that the swift years
Have passed by powerless o'er my unblanched
   hair.
  [*He moves with long strides across the Saloon, and re-
   mains on the opposite side over against* GORDON.
Who now persists in calling Fortune false?
To me she has proved faithful, with fond love
Took me from out the common ranks of men,
And like a mother goddess with strong arm
Carried me swiftly up the steps of life.
Nothing is common in my destiny,
Nor in the furrows of my hand. Who dares
Interpret then my life for me as 'twere
One of the undistinguishable many?
True in this present moment I appear
Fall'n low indeed; but I shall rise again.
The high flood will soon follow on this ebb;
The fountain of my fortune, which now stops
Repressed and bound by some malicious star,
Will soon in joy play forth from all its pipes.
 Gor. And yet remember I the good old proverb,
" Let the night come before we praise the day."

I would be slow from long continued fortune
To gather hope: for hope is the companion
Given to the unfortunate by pitying Heaven.
Fear hovers round the head of prosperous men;
For still unsteady are the scales of fate.   [of old

  Wal. [*smiling.*] I hear the very Gordon that
Was wont to preach to me, now once more
        preaching;
I know well, that all sublunary things
Are still the vassals of vicissitude.
The unpropitious gods demand their tribute.
This long ago the ancient Pagans knew:
And therefore of their own accord they offered
To themselves injuries, so to atone
The jealousy of their divinities:
And human sacrifices bled to Typhon.

    [*After a pause, serious, and in a more subdued manner.*
I too have sacrificed to him—For me
There fell the dearest friend, and through my
        fault
He fell! No joy from favourable fortune
Can overweigh the anguish of this stroke.
The envy of my destiny is glutted:
Life pays for life. On his pure head the lightning
Was drawn off which would else have shattered *me*.

      Scene III.—*To these enter* Seni.

  Wal. Is not that Seni? and beside himself,
If one may trust his looks! what brings thee
        hither

At this late hour, Baptista?
 Seni.   Terror, Duke!
On thy account.
 Wal.   What now?
 Seni.   Flee ere the day-break!
Trust not thy person to the Swedes!
 Wal.   What now
Is in thy thoughts?
 Seni. [*with louder voice.*] Trust not thy person
    to these Swedes!
 Wal.   What is it then?
 Seni. [*still more urgently.*] O wait not the arrival of these Swedes!
An evil near at hand is threatening thee
From false friends. All the signs stand full of
   horror!
Near, near at hand the net-work of perdition—
Yea, even now 'tis being cast around thee!
 Wal. Baptista, thou art dreaming!—Fear befools thee.   [me.
 Seni. Believe not that an empty fear deludes
Come, read it in the planetary aspects;
Read it thyself, that ruin threatens thee
From false friends!
 Wal.   From the falseness of my friends
Has risen the whole of my unprosperous fortunes.
The warning should have come before! At present
I need no revelation from the stars
To know that.
 Seni.   Come and see! trust thine own eyes!

A fearful sign stands in the house of life
An enemy; a fiend lurks close behind
The radiance of thy planet—O be warned!
Deliver not thyself up to these heathens
To wage a war against our holy church.

 Wal. [*laughing gently.*] The oracle rails that way! Yes, yes! Now
I recollect. This junction with the Swedes
Did never please thee—lay thyself to sleep,
Baptista! Signs like these I do not fear.

 Gor. [*who during the whole of this dialogue has shown marks of extreme agitation, and now turns to* WALLENSTEIN.] My Duke and General!
May I dare presume?

 Wal. Speak freely.

 Gor.   What if 'twere no mere creation
Of fear, if God's high providence vouchsafed
To interpose its aid for your deliverance,
And made that mouth its organ.

 Wal.   You're both feverish!
How can mishap come to me from the Swedes?
They sought this junction with me—'tis their interest.

 Gor. [*with difficulty suppressing his emotion.*]
    But what if the arrival of these Swedes—
What if this were the very thing that winged
The ruin that is flying to your temples?

        [*Flings himself at his feet.*
There is yet time, my Prince.

 Seni.   O hear him! hear him!

Gor. [*rises.*] The Rhinegrave's still far off.
        Give but the orders,
This citadel shall close its gates upon him.
If then he will besiege us, let him try it.
But this I say; he'll find his own destruction
With his whole force before these ramparts, sooner
Than weary down the valour of our spirit.
He shall experience what a band of heroes,
Inspirited by an heroic leader,
Is able to perform. And if indeed
It be thy serious wish to make amends
For that which thou hast done amiss,—this, this
Will touch and reconcile the Emperor.
Who gladly turns his heart to thoughts of mercy,
And Friedland, who returns repentant to him,
Will stand yet higher in his Emperor's favour,
Than e'er he stood when he had never fallen.

Wal. [*contemplates him with surprise, remains silent awhile, betraying strong emotion.*] Gordon—
       your zeal and fervour lead you far.
Well, well—an old friend has a privilege.
Blood, Gordon, has been flowing. Never, never
Can the Emperor pardon me: and if he could,
Yet I—I ne'er could let myself be pardoned.
Had I foreknown what now has taken place,
That he, my dearest friend would fall for me,
My first death-offering: and had the heart
Spoken to me, as now it has done—Gordon,
It may be I might have bethought myself.
It may be too, I might not. Might or might not,

Is now an idle question. All too seriously
Has it begun to end in nothing, Gordon!
Let it then have its course.
[*Stepping to the window.*
All dark and silent—at the castle too
All is now hushed—Light me Chamberlain!
  [*The* Groom of the Chamber, *who had entered during
  the last dialogue, and had been standing at a distance
  and listening to it with visible expressions of the
  deepest interest, advances in extreme agitation, and
  throws himself at the* DUKE'S *feet.*
And thou too! But I know why thou dost wish
My reconcilement with the Emperor.
Poor man! he hath a small estate in Cärnthen,
And fears it will be forfeited because
He's in my service. Am I then so poor,
That I no longer can indemnify
My servants. Well! To no one I employ
Means of compulsion. If 'tis thy belief
That fortune has fled from me, go! Forsake me.
This night for the last time mayst thou unrobe me,
And then go over to thy Emperor.
Gordon, good night! I think to make a long
Sleep of it: for the struggle and the turmoil
Of this last day or two were great. May't please
    you!
Take care that they awake me not too early.
  [*Exit* WALLENSTEIN, *the* Groom of the Chamber,
  lighting him. SENI *follows,* GORDON *remains on
  the darkened Stage following the* DUKE *with his eye
  till he disappears at the farther end of the gallery:
  then by his gestures the old man expresses the depth
  of his anguish, and stands leaning against a pillar.*

Scene IV.—Gordon, Butler (*at first behind the scenes.*)

But. [*not yet come into view of the stage.*]
　Here stand in silence till I give the signal.
Gor. [*starts up.*] 'Tis he, he has already
　brought the murderers.
But. The lights are out. All lies in profound
　sleep.
Gor. What shall I do, shall I attempt to save
　him?
Shall I call up the house? Alarm the guards?
But. [*appears, but scarcely on the stage.*] A
　light gleams hither from the corridor.
It leads directly to the Duke's bed-chamber.
Gor. But then I break my oath to the Empe-
　ror;
If he escape and strengthen the enemy,
Do I not hereby call down on my head
All the dread consequences?
But. [*stepping forward.*] Hark! Who speaks
　there?
Gor. 'Tis better, I resign it to the hands
Of Providence. For what am I, that *I*
Should take upon myself so great a deed?
I have not murdered him, if he be murdered;
But all his rescue were *my* act and deed;
Mine—and whatever be the consequences,
I must sustain them.
But. [*advances.*] I should know that voice.

Gor. Butler!

But. 'Tis Gordon. What do *you* want here?
Was it so late then when the Duke dismissed you?

Gor. Your hand bound up and in a scarf?

But.   'Tis wounded.
That Illo fought as he was frantic, till
At last we threw him on the ground.

Gor. [*shuddering.*]   Both dead?

But. Is he in bed?

Gor.   Ah, Butler!

But.   Is he? speak.

Gor. He shall *not* perish! not through you!
    The Heaven
Refuses *your* arm. See—'tis wounded!—

But. There is no need of *my* arm.

Gor.   The most guilty
Have perished, and enough is given to justice.

    [*The* Groom of the Chamber *advances from the gallery
        with his finger on his mouth commanding silence.*

He sleeps! O murder not the holy sleep!

But. No! he shall die awake.   [*is going.*

Gor.   His heart still cleaves
To earthly things: he's not prepared to step
Into the presence of his God!

But. [*going.*]   God's merciful!

Gor. [*holds him.*] Grant him but this night's
    respite.

But. [*hurrying off.*]   The next moment
May ruin all.

Gor. [*holds him still.*] One hour!——
But. Unhold me! What
can that short respite profit him?
Gor. O—Time
works miracles. In one hour many thousands
Of grains of sand run out; and quick as they,
Thought follows thought within the human soul.
Only one hour! *Your* heart may change its pur-
    pose,
His heart may change its purpose—some new
    tidings
May come: some fortunate event, decisive,
May fall from Heaven and rescue him. O what
May not one hour achieve!
But. You but remind me,
How precious every minute is!
                  [*He stamps on the floor.*

SCENE V.—*To these enter* MACDONALD *and* DEVEREUX,
      with the Halberdiers.

Gor. [*throwing himself between him and them.*]
No, monster!
First over my dead body thou shalt tread.
I will not live to see the accursed deed!
But. [*forcing him out of the way.*] Weak-
    hearted dotard!
        [*Trumpets are heard in the distance.*
Dev. and Mac. Hark! the Swedish trumpets!

The Swedes before the ramparts! Let us hasten!

Gor. [*rushes out.*] O God of Mercy!

But. [*calling after him.*] Governor to your post!

Groom of the Chamber. [*hurries in.*] Who dares make larum here? Hush! The Duke sleeps.

Dev. [*with loud harsh voice.*] Friend, it is time now to make larum.

Groom of the Chamber. Help! Murder!

But. Down with him!

Groom of the Chamber. [*run through the body by* DEVEREUX, *falls at the entrance of the gallery.*] Jesus Maria!

But. Burst the doors open!

[*They rush over the body into the gallery—two doors are heard to crash one after the other—Voices deadened by the distance—Clash of arms—then all at once a profound silence.*

SCENE VI.—COUNTESS TERTSKY (*with a light.*)

Her bed-chamber is empty; she herself
Is nowhere to be found! The Neubrunn too,
Who watched by her, is missing. If she should
Be flown—But whither flown? We must call up
Every soul in the house. How will the Duke
Bear up against these worst bad tidings? O

If that my husband now were but returned
Home from the banquet: Hark! I wonder
    whether
The Duke is still awake! I thought I heard
Voices and tread of feet here! I will go
And listen at the door. Hark! What is that?
'Tis hastening up the steps!

    SCENE VII.—COUNTESS, GORDON.

Gor. [*rushes in out of breath.*] 'Tis a mistake,
'Tis not the Swedes—Ye must proceed no fur-
    ther—
Butler! O God! Where is he?
               [*Then observing the* COUNTESS.
              Countess! Say——
  Coun. You are come then from the castle?
    Where's my husband?
  Gor. [*in an agony of affright.*] Your husband!
—Ask not!—To the Duke——
  Coun.   Not till
You have discovered to me——
  Gor.   On this moment
Does the world hang. For God's sake! to the
    Duke.
While we are speaking——   [*Calling loudly.*
            Butler! Butler! God!
  Coun. Why, he is at the castle with my husband.
              [BUTLER *comes from the gallery.*

Gor. 'Twas a mistake—'Tis not the Swedes—it is
The Imperialist's Lieutenant-General
Has sent me hither, will be here himself
Instantly.—You must not proceed.

But.   He comes
Too late.   [GORDON *dashes himself against the wall.*

Gor. O God of mercy!

Coun.   What, too late?
Who will be here himself?   Octavio
In Egra?   Treason!   Treason!   Where's the
    Duke?   [*She rushes to the gallery.*

SCENE VIII.—*Servants run across the Stage full of terror. The whole Scene must be spoken entirely without pauses.*

Seni. [*from the gallery.*]   O bloody frightful
    deed!

Coun.   What is it, Seni?

Page. [*from the gallery.*]   O piteous sight!
            [*Other* Servants *hasten in with torches.*

Coun. What is it?   For God's sake!

Seni.   And do *you* ask?
Within the Duke lies murdered—and your husband
Assassinated at the Castle.
            [*The* COUNTESS *stands motionless.*

Female Servant. [*rushing across the Stage.*]
    Help! Help! the Duchess!

Burgomaster. [*enters.*] What mean these confused
Loud cries, that wake the sleepers of this house?
Gor. Your house is cursed to all eternity.
In your house doth the Duke lie murdered!
Bur. [*rushing out.*] Heaven forbid!
1st Ser. Fly! fly! they murder us all!
2d Ser. [*carrying silver plate.*] That way! The lower
Passages are blocked up.
Voice from behind the Scene. Make room for the Lieutenant-General!

[*At these words the* COUNTESS *starts from her stupor, collects herself, and retires suddenly.*

Voice from behind the Scene. Keep back the people! Guard the door.

SCENE IX.—*To these enters* OCTAVIO PICCOLOMINI *with all his train. At the same time* DEVEREUX *and* MACDONALD *enter from out the Corridor with the* Halberdiers. WALLENSTEIN'S *dead body is carried over the back part of the Stage, wrapped in a piece of crimson tapestry.*

Oct. [*entering abruptly.*] It must not be! It is not possible!
Butler! Gordon!
 I'll not believe it. Say no!
[GORDON, *without answering, points with his hand to the body of* WALLENSTEIN *as it is carried over the back of the Stage.* OCTAVIO *looks that way, and stands overpowered with horror.*

Dev. [*to* Butler.] Here is the golden fleece—
 the Duke's sword—
Mac. Is it your order—
But. [*pointing to* Octavio.] Here stands he
 who now
Hath the sole power to issue orders.

 [Devereux *and* Macdonald *retire with marks of
  obeisance. One drops away after the other, till only
  *Butler, Octavio, *and* Gordon *remain on the
  Stage.*

 Oct. [*turning to* Butler.] Was that my pur-
  pose, Butler, when we parted?
O God of Justice
To thee I lift my hand! I am not guilty
Of this foul deed.
 But.   Your *hand* is pure. You have
Availed yourself of mine.
 Oct.   Merciless man!
Thus to abuse the orders of thy Lord—
And stain thy Emperor's holy name with murder,
With bloody, most accursed assassination!
 But. [*calmly.*] I've but fulfilled the Emperor's
  own sentence.
 Oct. O curse of kings,
Infusing a dread life into their words,
And linking to the sudden transient thought
The unchangeable irrevocable deed.
Was there necessity for such an eager
Despatch? Couldst thou not grant the merciful
A time for mercy? Time is man's good angel.

THE DEATH OF WALLENSTEIN.   323

To leave no interval between the sentence,
And the fulfilment of it, doth beseem
God only, the immutable!
   But.   For what
Rail you against me? What is my offence?
The Empire from a fearful enemy
Have I delivered, and expect reward.
The single difference 'twixt you and me
Is this: you placed the arrow in the bow,
I pulled the string. You sowed blood, and yet stand
Astonished that blood is come up. I always
Knew what I did, and therefore no result
Hath power to frighten or surprise my spirit.
Have you aught else to order?—for this instant
I make my best speed to Vienna; place
My bleeding sword before my Emperor's throne,
And hope to gain the applause which undelaying
And punctual obedience may demand
From a just judge.   [*Exit* BUTLER.

SCENE X.—*To these enter the* COUNTESS TERTSKY, *pale and disordered. Her utterance is slow and feeble, and unimpassioned.*

   Oct. [*meeting her.*] O Countess Tertsky! These are the results
Of luckless unblest deeds.
   Coun.   They are the fruits
Of your contrivances. The Duke is dead.

My husband too is dead, the Duchess struggles
In the pangs of death, my niece has disappeared.
This house of splendour and of princely glory,
Doth now stand desolated: the affrighted servants
Rush forth through all its doors. I am the last
Therein; I shut it up, and here deliver
The keys.
    Oct. [*with deep anguish.*] O Countess! my
        house too is desolate.
    Coun. Who next is to be murdered? Who is
        next
To be maltreated? Lo! The Duke is dead.
The Emperor's vengeance may be pacified!
Spare the old servants; let not their fidelity
Be imputed to the faithful as a crime—
The evil destiny surprised my brother
Too suddenly: he could not think on them.
    Oct. Speak not of vengeance! Speak not of
        maltreatment!
The Emp'ror is appeased; the heavy fault
Hath heavily been expiated—nothing
Descended from the father to the daughter,
Except his glory and his services.
The Empress honours your adversity,
Takes part in your afflictions, opens to you
Her motherly arms! Therefore no farther fears!
Yield yourself up in hope and confidence
To the Imperial Grace!
    Coun. [*with her eye raised to heaven.*] To the
        grace and mercy of a greater Master

Do I yield up myself. Where shall the body
Of the Duke have its place of final rest?
In the Chartreuse, which he himself did found
At Gitschin, rests the Countess Wallenstein;
And by her side, to whom he was indebted
For his first fortunes, gratefully he wished
He might sometime repose in death! O let him
Be buried there. And likewise, for my husband's
Remains, I ask the like grace. The Emperor
Is now proprietor of all our castles.
This sure may well be granted us—one sepulchre
Beside the sepulchres of our forefathers!

Oct. Countess, you tremble, you turn pale!
Coun. [*reassembles all her powers, and speaks
with energy and dignity.*] You think
More worthily of me, than to believe
I would survive the downfall of my house.
We did not hold ourselves too mean to grasp
After a monarch's crown—the crown did fate
Deny, but not the feeling and the spirit
That to the crown belong! We deem a
Courageous death more worthy of our free station
Than a dishonoured life.—I have taken poison.

Oct. Help! Help! Support her!
Coun. Nay, it is too late.
In a few moments is my fate accomplished.

[*Exit* COUNTESS.

Gor. O house of death and horrors!
[*An officer enters, and brings a letter with the great seal.*
Gor. [*steps forward and meets him.*] What is
this?

It is the Imperial Seal.

> [*He reads the address, and delivers the letter to* OCTAVIO *with a look of reproach, and with an emphasis on the word.*

To the Prince Piccolomini.

> [OCTAVIO *with his whole frame expressive of sudden anguish, raises his eyes to heaven.*

The curtain drops.

NOTES TO THE TRANSLATION,

REPRINTED FROM THE FIRST EDITION.

Page 161, line 1.
This age and after-ages speak my name.

COULD I have hazarded such a Germanism, as the use of the word after-world for posterity,—"Es spreche Welt und Nachwelt meinen Nahmen" might have been rendered with more literal fidelity:—Let world and after-world speak out my name, &c.

Page 161, line 12.
Make thy flesh shudder, and thy whole heart sicken.

I have not ventured to affront the fastidious delicacy of our age with a literal translation of this line—

"werth
Die Eingeweide schaudernd aufzuregen."

(This is omitted in the German as it now stands.—D. C.)

Page 240, line 20.

I have here ventured to omit a considerable number of lines. I fear that I should not have done amiss had I taken this liberty more frequently. It is, however, incumbent on me to give the original with a literal translation:—

Weh denen die auf dich vertraun, an dich
Die sich're Hütte ihres Glückes lehnen,
Gelockt von deiner gastlichen Gestalt!
Schnell, unverhofft, bei nächtlich stiller Weile
Gährt's in dem tück'schen Feuerschlunde, ladet
Sich aus mit tobender Gewalt, und weg
Treibt über alle Pflanzungen der Menschen
Der wilde Strom in grausender zerstöhrung.

WALLENSTEIN.

Du schilderst deines Vaters Herz. Wie du's
Beschreibst so ists in seinem Einge weide,
In dieser schwarzen Heuchler-Brust gestaltet.
O mich hat Höllenkunst getäuscht. Mir sandte
Der Abgrund den verstecktesten der Geister,
Den lügekundigsten herauf, und stellt' ihn
Als Freund an meine Seite. Wer vermag
Der Hölle Macht zu widerstehn! Ich zog
Den Basilisken auf an meinem Busen,
Mit meinem Herzblut nährt ich ihn, er sog
Sich schwelgend voll an meiner Liebe Brüsten,
Ich hatte nimmer Arges gegen ihn,
Weit offen liess ich des Gedankens Thore,
Und warf die Schlüssel weiser Vorsicht weg,
Am Sternenhimmel, &c.

LITERAL TRANSLATION.

Alas! for those who place their confidence on thee, against thee lean the secure hut of their fortune, allured by thy hospitable form. Suddenly, unexpectedly, in a moment still as night, there is a fermentation in the treacherous gulf of fire; it discharges itself with raging force, and away over all the plantations of men drives the wild stream in frightful devastation.

WALLENSTEIN.

Thou art portraying thy father's heart. As thou describest, even so is it shaped in his entrails, in this black hypocrite's breast. O, the art of hell has deceived me! The abyss sent up to me the most spotted of the spirits, the most skilful in lies, and placed him as a friend at my side. Who may withstand the power of hell? I took the basilisk to my bosom, with my heart's blood I nourished him; he sucked himself glut-full at the breasts of my love. I never harboured evil towards him; wide open did I leave the door of my thoughts; I threw away the key of wise foresight. In the starry heaven, &c.

We find a difficulty in believing this to have been written by Schiller.

The following notes are from the pen of the late lamented Mrs. H. N. Coleridge, the editor's sister, who was engaged in an examination of the translation of Wallenstein with a view to this edition, which she did not live to complete:—

Note 1.

About a year and a half ago, a writer in " The Westminster Review" undertook to prove that the world had been mistaken all those years—from 1800 to 1850, that is, half a century—in imagining that it had obtained from the pen of Coleridge a translation of Schiller's Wallenstein, creditable to English literature, both from its poetical merit, and its general fidelity to the spirit of the original work. On the contrary, this critic, who signs himself G. H. E., endeavours to show that " it would have been better for the poet, for the reader, and for the credit of the translator, had Mr. C. refrained from meddling with the work, or confined himself to the task of a faithful interpretation."

In pursuance of this enterprise, he brings forward a certain number of unquestionable errors in the sense of the German; errors, doubtless, well known from the first to students of Schiller, and admirers of Coleridge, (that the report of them reached the German author himself, together with the first news that his noble play had been done into English, we are credibly informed by one who had a personal acquaintance with him,) and which have not been hitherto generally supposed to prevent Mr. Coleridge's version from being, on the whole, a highly meritorious performance. Of these errors we shall proceed to lay a list before the reader; premising, however, that the greater number of substitutions to be found in Mr. C.'s pages are not, as G. H. E. pronounces them, mere imbecility and verbiage, but contain a sufficiently pertinent meaning, and make up, in a homelier liveliness, what they lack of Schiller's sedate dignity—that of some others the worst that can be said is, that the meaning is strained and far-sought; and that there are but a few instances in which, it must be confessed, the translator has trespassed against good sense, as well as forgotten the German language:—

"Brimful of poetry, o'er the briny ocean, home
Soon he fell a nodding—at our house at home.
Nid nid nodding—at our house at home."

Note 2.

We now proceed to give a list of verbal errors in Mr. Coleridge's version: the translation has remained entirely unaltered from the first edition to the last.

West. Review, July, 1850. Art. 3.

Page 353: "Der Posten," rendered "travelling-bills," instead of an "item" or "article in an account."
PICC., SCH., COL.—*Act* i. *Scene* 2.

Page 353: "Geschmeidig" "pliant," mistaken for "geschmiedet," "hammered out."
PICC., SCH., COL.—*Act* i. *Scene* 4.

Pages 356-7: "Jagdzug," rendered "hunting-dress," instead of "hunting-stud." PICC., SCH., COL.—*Act* i. *Scene* 9.

Page 358: "Das holde kind!" translated "The voice of my child!" a bold substitution for "The charming child."
PICC., SCH., COL.—*Act* i. *Scene* 8.

Page 360: "Was denn?" "What *then?*" instead of "What?"
PICC., SCH., COL.—*Act* ii. *Scene* 7.

Page 361: "Ist unser Glaub' um Kanzel und Altar," rendered "Our faith hangs upon the pulpit and altar," instead of "is without pulpit and altar."
PICC., SCH., COL.—*Act* ii. *Scene* 12.

Page 362: "Losung," "watchword," mistaken for "Erlösung," "redemption."
SCH., WALL., COL.—*Act* iv. *Scene* 7.

Page 365: "Verstecktesten" most secret," mistaken for "beflecktesten," "most spotted." NOTES, p. 329.

THE END.

3274289

Made in the USA